Cable Car

Confidential

by Susan Holtzer

To Mat –
with special thanks.
— Susan Holtzer

Cable Car Confidential:
Outrageous, Absolutely True Stories from San Francisco Gripmen
by Susan Holtzer

Published by Cable Car Books
Caddo Gap Press
3145 Geary Boulevard PMB 275
San Francisco, California 94118

Copyright 2002
by Caddo Gap Press

ISBN 1-880192-40-3

$14.95

Library of Congress Cataloging-in-Publication Data

Holtzer, Susan, 1940-
  Cable car confidential : outrageous, absolutely true stories from San
Francisco gripmen / by Susan Holtzer.
      p. cm.
  ISBN 1-880192-40-3 (alk. paper)
  1. Railroads, Cable. 2. Street-railroads—California—San Francisco.
I. Title.
  TF835 .H65 2002
  388.4'6'0979461—dc21

                                2002000981

Table of Contents

Changing the grip
of a California line cable car

Author's Note 5

Glossary 6

Stupid Cable Car Tricks 7

Only in San Francisco 18

"We Don't Do Curb Service" 27

The Tower 40

Sex and the Cable Cars 47

The Gripman's Way 58

The Learning Curve 73

Silly Gripmen's Tricks 82

Conductors 93

Us vs. Them 102

Dedication

This book is dedicated with gratitude to the knights of the rope, especially . . . well, you know who you are. Because if I mentioned names I'd have to move out of San Francisco, and I'll never, ever do that.

Author's Note

This book is a work of pure serendipity. That is, it's not a book I set out purposely to write; rather, it's a book that just sort of happened to me.

I mean, I started riding the cable cars, and the guys started telling me these stories. And after a while... Well, what's an author to do when a book climbs up her leg demanding her attention?

Is this account opinionated and maybe more than a little one-sided? Sure it is. This book is about — and for — the gripmen and conductors who keep the cable cars running. If someone wants to do a book about those wonderful, caring fellows in Muni management, by all means go for it.

I have one more person to thank, besides the dozens of gripmen and conductors who participated in this book. That's a terrific author/editor/teacher/all-around-great-person named Shelley Singer, who went through the early manuscript, laughed — or didn't — and told me why, and kept asking "what on earth does that mean?" until I got it properly explained.

A note about paranoia:

Because everyone who was good enough to participate in this book was guaranteed absolute confidentiality, I've gone to extreme lengths to protect that promise.

Thus, every single name in this book is fictitious. *Every* name. Too, names have been changed from anecdote to anecdote. That is, if a particular operator related three different stories, or offered three different comments, they're related here under three different fictitious names.

There's one exception, and that's Jake. No, Jake isn't his real name; but all the stories about Jake are about one single, singular, unique guy. You couldn't make it all up if you tried.

And one more thing — in most cases I don't know, myself, who told me which stories. In the process of gathering material, I tape-recorded a series of interviews. As each tape was filled, I transcribed it without identifying the speakers, then re-used the tapes for new interviews. So don't even bother to ask who told me what, because the honest truth is, most of the time I don't know myself.

Because a little paranoia never hurts.

Glossary

Slot blade, throwing a blade: The slot blade is the red-handled emergency brake at the front of the cable car. Pulling the handle drives a metal wedge into the slot the cable runs through, bringing the car to an immediate halt. Gripmen refer to this as "throwing a blade."

Track brake: Pulling the track brake lever stops the car by forcing four pieces of soft wood against the metal tracks.

Wheel brake: Metal braking shoes that are forced against the wheels. The wheel brakes are operated by foot pedals.

Rope, cable: Interchangeable terms for the underground cable that pulls the cars.

Dropping the rope: Releasing the cable from the grip, either purposely or by accident.

Strand: One of the individual wires that are twisted to make up the cable. A broken strand brings the line to a halt until it's repaired.

Inbound/outbound: toward/away from downtown. On the Powell lines, "inbound" means toward Market Street; on the California line, it means toward Drumm Street and the Embarcadero.

The tower: The small building at California and Powell whose function is traffic control.

RDO: Regular Day Off. A gripman "working RDO" is working overtime.

On industrial: An operator "on industrial" is out because of injury or illness.

Let-go: There are several points along all cable car lines where the gripman has to release the cable from the grip. These points are called "let-go's;" gripmen refer to the maneuver as "making a let-go."

Take-rope: Once past the let-go, the gripman has to pick up the cable again. These are referred to as "take-rope" points.

Bumper bar: An underground barrier to prevent the grip from running into the cable if the gripman misses the let-go.

Skinning the rope: Opening the grip slightly to let the cable slide through it, in order to increase speed going downhill.

Stupid Cable Car Tricks

Everyone who comes to San Francisco wants to ride the cable cars, just as everyone who goes to Disneyland wants to ride the teacups. The trouble is, the SF Visitors Bureau notwithstanding, San Francisco isn't a theme park, and the cable cars aren't a carnival ride.

What they are, once you get past the terminally quaint adorableness of it all, is public transit. And the dirty little secret of cable cars is this: However charming it looks in the movies, like nearly all urban public transportation, riding cables cars is uncomfortable.

The purpose of the exercise, after all, isn't providing tourists with an excursion; its purpose is simply moving as many people as possible from Point A to Point B. Comfort and scenery are optional extras, depending on the luck of the draw.

One of the ways more passengers cram onto cable cars, of course, is by standing on the running board. This is a tradition that goes

7

Printed between each pair
of poles, beneath
the running board.

back to the very earliest days of cable cars, and over the decades, a set of run-ning-board regulations and etiquette has evolved:

- It is Not Okay to complain if someone standing in front of you blocks your view.
- Corollary: If you're standing in front of someone, it is polite to move aside briefly for photo ops.
- It is Not Okay to cross your legs in an attempt to keep passengers from standing in front of you.
- On a crowded car, packages, purses, and coats go on your lap or tucked well back on the floor behind your feet, not on the seat next to you.
- By Muni regulation, for reasons of safety, only two people are permitted to stand on the running board between each pair of posts. It is Never Okay to cram an extra person in with the airy comment: "Oh, that's all right, we can squeeze in."
- On the other hand, it is also Not Okay to refuse to move over when some-one wants to board in that second spot between your two poles. It is especially Not Okay to use your backpack, purse, or derriere to signal your displeasure by ramming them backward against the pole.
- And finally: It is Never Okay to sing the Rice-a-Roni jingle on a cable car. Never. Ever.

The public transit aspect of the cable cars can be a difficult concept, espe-cially for tourists.

Now, San Francisco gets probably the best tourists in the world. They are, by and large, cheerful, polite, well-behaved, and a pleasure to have around.

They are also often lost, confused, and utterly bewildered — especially by cable cars.

Cable cars have no outside equivalent. San Francisco traffic may be terrifying, but at least they've seen traffic before. Ditto the towering hills. Tourists may be fascinated, or frightened, or delighted by other San Francisco attractions, but at least they understand them. Cable cars are utterly unique, and to many tourists, utterly incomprehensible as anything but a kind of carnival ride.

That's what the middle-aged woman in the purple warmup togs figured.

She'd stood in line at Powell and Market for nearly an hour, but she and her friend had scored seats on the outside bench and she was feeling quite pleased with herself. That is, she was until half a dozen people — who obviously *hadn't* stood in the long, tedious line — boarded the cable car at O'Farrell. She looked at her friend in annoyance but said nothing. The car stopped at Geary, where several more people got on, and she looked even more annoyed.

Finally, when even more passengers climbed aboard at Post Street, she couldn't contain herself. Glaring at the people in front of her on the running board, she said loudly to her friend: "How come they just let people jump on at every corner whenever they want to?"

🚋 🚋 🚋

Then there was the woman who subscribed to the Zoo Train theory. She approached the gripman at California and Drumm, the eastern terminus of the Cal line.

"Where does this car go?" she asked sweetly.

"It goes down California Street to Van Ness Avenue," the gripman explained. "Seventeen blocks down, and seventeen blocks back."

The woman thought this through for a while. Finally, she asked: "Does it stop anywhere along the way?"

The California Street line, in fact, is still basic transportation for many locals in the area. The line, which runs from Van Ness Avenue at the edge of Pacific Heights, up and over Nob Hill and down to the Financial District, is particularly busy during the morning rush hour. At 8:30 in the morning, every car on the line is in service, all of them jammed with commuters. And at 8:30 in the morning, tourists flat-out aren't welcome, except maybe for the occasional comic relief.

The middle-aged woman was sweet and cheerful and unbearably chatty for 8:30 in the morning. She was anxious for conversation with "real San Franciscans;" the real San Franciscans only wanted to read their Wall Street Journals, mainline their caffeine, and get to work. Finally the woman asked brightly: "What do you people do when it rains?"

And without any prompting, a dozen commuters replied in almost perfect unison: "We get wet!"

She was well-dressed and well-groomed and didn't look particularly like a tourist. She boarded the car at Stockton near the end of the rush hour, her high-heeled shoes planted comfortably on the running board.

"Fare, please." Jamal, the conductor, extended his hand.

"Excuse me?" she said politely.

"Fare, please," Jamal repeated.

The woman looked at him in surprise. "You mean you have to pay to ride the cable cars?"

"Yes, ma'am." Jamal kept a straight face, while the locals looked at each other and stifled grins. "Two dollars one way, six dollars for an all-day pass."

"Oh, goodness." The woman hitched her purse on her shoulder and stepped off the car. "I don't want to *pay*." And as the locals broke down laughing, she said crossly, "I thought the cable cars were just something that San Francisco provided for tourists."

Tourists with children are especially likely to fall victim to the Zoo Train theory. Otherwise conscientious parents, who wouldn't even take their eyes off their children in a suburban shopping mall, somehow block out the dangers of riding cable cars — the racketing traffic pouring past on both sides, the jerky motion that makes riding on the running board a balancing act, the fact that gripmen are far too busy to serve as babysitters.

Item: The parents — and there are legions of them — who calmly go inside the compartment and sit down, leaving their five- and six-year-olds to stand on the running board by themselves.

Item: The parents who laughed appreciatively when their ten-year-old stood up on the bench to reach for the bell cord and was grabbed by the gripman just as the child was about to plunge into the grip hole.

Item: The parents who got into a shouting match with the gripman who

The signs say "Keep Off Tracks," of course...

wouldn't permit the father to stand on the running board with a six-month-old baby strapped to his back in a papoose carrier.

Particularly clueless was the father who popped his five-year-old on the running board, left him there, and jumped into his car, idling next to the tracks. His plan? To drive alongside the cable car videotaping the child's ride.

And then there was the father who figured his kid could be his ticket to ride.

He was part of a scrum of passengers trying to board a Wharf-bound cable car at Sutter and Powell, and it was pretty clear they weren't all going to get on. Warren, the conductor, counted them off: "We've got room for four more — you, you, you, and you." He pointed; the father wasn't one of them.

Warren saw the man mutter something to the small boy, and give him a slight push. As the chosen four crammed themselves onto the cable car, the boy squeezed in with them.

Warren spread his arms across the doorway. "that's it, folks; we're full." And to the gripman: "Two bells" (bell code for the all-clear.)

"Wait!" the father called out, waving his arms. "I have to get on! My kid's on the car!"

"Your kid's on the car?" Warren played dumb.

"Yes, he's inside." The father put a foot on the step.

Warren stepped in front of him. "That's okay, we'll get him out. Come on out, young man," he called into the compartment. And as the father glowered on the pavement: "You don't want to let him ride alone, do you?"

And then there are the legions of the Generally Clueless.

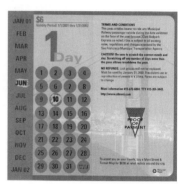

The Muni three-day Passport, which is good on buses, streetcars, and cable cars, is nothing more than a scratch-off calendar. You get to pick any three consecutive days you want; if you're riding on, say, June 10, you scratch off the silver overlay that says "June," and the silver overlay that says "10."

It's hard to imagine a more idiot-proof system — if only idiots weren't so amazingly inventive.

The little blonde was young and giggly and working hard at flirting with the good-looking conductor. She flashed the Passport archly and tossed her head.

"You've got to scratch off the date." Terrell, the conductor, enjoyed the flirting, but he did want to get on with collecting fares.

"What do you mean?" She looked from Terrell to the Passport without comprehension.

"You scratch off the month, and then the date." Terrell couldn't figure out how to make it any clearer.

The blonde frowned at the Passport for a while, and finally her face lit up. "Oh, I get it!" she said happily. "What's today's date?"

"February 12," Terrell said.

The blonde scratched away at the Passport and after several minutes held it up triumphantly. "There."

She'd scratched off the "February" okay. Only, instead of scratching off the "12" under February, she'd scratched off the "1" and the "2."

At top speed, cable cars go only nine and a half miles an hour. But speed and acceleration are different things. Zero-to-9-1/2 in one second can rip the grip out of a gripman's hand and send passengers flying off the car like runaway pinballs. Gripmen call this truly dangerous phenomenon a Jump; one of the first things they're taught, in training, is how to ease the grip onto the cable, and ease the car forward smoothly.

The Japanese tourist, clearly, didn't know anything about Jumps. He stood in

A gripman pushes his cable car off the turntable at Powell and Market.

line with his tour group at Powell and Market, watching as the cable car was pushed off the turntable.

The turntables, like everything else about the cable cars, are operated by muscle, not machinery. First, the car is driven onto the table. When it's brought to a stop, both the gripman and the conductor jump off, grab the turntable's metal handrails, and wrestle the mechanism around until the car is facing the other direction. Then they push it off the table. They do this from the rear, by brute force, putting their backs against the back of the car and pushing with their legs, basically walking the car off the turntable and letting it glide up to the loading point.

Here, the cable is high in the slot; the grip is always pushed all the way forward, which keeps it up and away from the cable. All the gripman needs to do is pull back on the grip handle to engage the cable.

And here, for the space of a few seconds, the cable car is unattended.

Omar's empty car came to a stop at the loading gate, and people began to board. Omar hopped onto the back and took one casual step forward. That's when he spotted the tourist, pushing past the other passengers, squeezing into the slot between the benches, and reaching for the grip.

"Hey!" Omar let out a shout, but he didn't wait for a reaction. Instinctively, he launched himself forward, through the compartment to the front of the car, and rammed into the back of the tourist in the slot. The impact shoved the tourist chest-first against the grip, knocking it forward as well and raising it out of the way of the cable.

"What the hell were you thinking?" Omar shouted at him. The tourist mumbled something in Japanese, picked himself up and fled. The other passengers eyed Omar nervously and muttered to each other. Then a couple of them seemed to recall previous appointments and hurriedly got off he car.

They'd never heard of a Jump, either, but they were pretty sure they didn't want to ride with a crazy gripman who hurled himself at his passengers.

🚋 🚋 🚋

The woman boarded the car at the Market Street turntable, standing on the back deck and peering around with bright-eyed interest. "Where does this go?" she asked the conductor.

"Down to Beach and Hyde, at Ghirardelli Square," Monty replied.

"Does it come back?" she asked.

"Oh no, ma'am." Monty decided to have some fun. "These are very old, and what we've been doing is, when we get down to the end we burn them." He grinned at her. "After I finish collecting the fares, I can sell you marshmallows."

The woman didn't return his grin. Instead, after a moment's thought she replied seriously, "Oh, okay."

Monty shook his head in disbelief, went through the car and collected fares, and returned to the back. The woman was still standing there, a pensive expression on her face. Not until the cable car was halfway up the hill did the light dawn.

"Oh, you!" She rapped him playfully on the arm. "You were putting me on, weren't you?"

Sometimes tourists are so fascinated with San Francisco that they forget the locals are real people, not Disney characters placed there for entertainment value. They'll happily ask the most personal and intrusive questions, the kind they would never ask a perfect stranger back in their home towns.

A sample of questions asked of locals by tourists on cable cars:

✄ To a commuter on the Cal line: "It's so expensive here. How much rent do you pay?"
✄ To a young man with an abstract tattoo on his hand: "Is that a Satanic symbol?"
✄ To a man with two diamond studs in his left ear: "Do those earrings mean you're gay?"

Cable cars can be confusing to tourists even when they're not trying to ride on them. Take someone from a small city or a suburb; put them behind the wheel of a rental car in a strange city of hills and tortuous street patterns; throw them into the whirling maelstrom of San Francisco traffic. Now add the peculiarities of the cable car system, and sit back and watch the fun.

At one end of each cable car line is a waiting area, where cable cars line up, one behind the other, waiting their turn to head back out. This waiting line is always on the *incoming* track.

Now, because cable cars travel down the middle of the street, inevitably traffic stacks up behind them until they reach this terminus. Here, finally, automobiles can pull out and go around them.

That is, if the driver knows it's the end of the line.

Like everything else about cable cars, however, there's nothing obvious about it. And so, on a regular basis, drivers — often two or three in a row — who've been following a cable car will remain in place behind it when it stops at the end of the line, patiently sitting ... and sitting ... and sitting ...

Sometimes gripmen will wave them around. Sometimes they'll take bets on how long a driver will sit before the light bulb goes on ...

Apparently, there's something mesmerizing about trailing behind a cable car for block after endless block. At nine and a half miles an hour, it's easy to stop paying attention and slip into autopilot.

At least, how else explain the woman in the rented Chevy?

She'd been trailing the cable car down Powell Street all the way from California, stopping at every intersection, waiting at every traffic jam. At last, the cable car trundled across Ellis to the brick-paved plaza — closed to automobile traffic — and headed for the turntable.

The Chevy's driver didn't notice the big "No Entry" signs. She didn't notice the barricades surrounding the plaza. Instead, she trundled right along behind the cable car, saw an opening — finally! — and swept past, right onto the cable car turntable.

🚋 🚋 🚋

It was a minor fender-bender at California and Montgomery of the all-too-common kind — a driver who'd cut in front of the cable car and clipped her rear bumper. Buck waited at the grip, as he was supposed to do, while the police took her statement.

Suddenly, he realized that the cop was doubled over laughing. Curious, he set the grip and hopped down off the car.

As he approached the angry driver and the laughing cop, he heard the woman say: "I'm telling you, it was not my fault." She pointed to the cable car idling on its tracks. "That thing swerved into my lane."

🚋 🚋 🚋

Then there was the woman who double-parked in front of the Sir Francis Drake Hotel on Powell.

She was blocking the tracks, so Scott stopped behind her and rang his bell. Nothing happened. He rang the bell again. The driver's window rolled down, and an arm appeared.

And the woman irritably signalled the cable car to go around her.

🚋 🚋 🚋

Gil still can't believe it actually went to court.

His cable car was just cresting the Jackson hill at Taylor when the Volkswagen ran the stop sign and pulled out into the intersection. Cable car met bug, and bug lost. Total damage was a medium-sized dent in the Volkswagen's fender.

Muni, as usual, wrote this up as operator error and agreed to repair the fender, but the driver wasn't satisfied. She demanded that they re-paint the entire car; when Muni refused, she went to small claims court asking for the maximum $1500.

"When I pulled into the intersection," she told the court, "the cable car was at the bottom of the hill. And just when I got ready to move, he rushed up the hill, came through the intersection and slammed into my car. He was racing up the hill, and I could hear the people on the car screaming for him to stop," she added for verisimilitude.

The judge turned to Gil. "What do you have to say about the accident?" he asked.

"Well, your honor," Gil carefully avoided laughing, "I'd just like to make the point that a cable car's top speed is only nine and a half miles an hour."

"And she didn't get anything at all," Gil reports. "Not even the dent repaired."

Even when there's no cable car in sight, the tracks alone pose their own unique difficulties. The gauge is a problem, for one thing; if you're driving on a street with cable car tracks, you have to position your car so that one set of wheels is between the tracks, which throws you slightly across traffic lanes.

And when it rains, they get slippery. Very slippery...

The BMW was halfway up the Jackson Street hill between Mason and Taylor, just past the cable car barn itself, when it unaccountably stopped moving. The young woman driver trod hard on the accelerator; from the top of the hill, you could hear the tortured squeal of tires and smell the stench of burning rubber, but the car refused to move.

She got out of the car, elegant in a suit and high heels, holding her umbrella high against the persistent rain. She walked around the car, peered at it from all angles. Meanwhile, traffic was backing up behind her on the one-lane street. Drivers began honking; at the bottom of the hill, a cable car clanged it's bell irritably.

She got back into the BMW and once more attempted to get it moving; once more squealing tires and burning rubber were the only result. Finally the woman stepped out of the car, waved her arms angrily at the honking drivers behind her, and took out her cell phone. She spoke anxiously into it, motioning at the car and shrugging, as if to say: I don't know, it just won't move.

Finally, a man in Muni blue trotted out of the cable car barn, his expression a mixture of exasperation and hilarity. He spoke to her for a minute or two, jerking his thumb at the offending Beamer. The woman looked startled, then defensive. She spoke into the cell phone for a minute, then closed it and trotted back to her car.

At which point she turned the steering wheel hard to the right, drove the BMW *off* the wet and slippery cable car tracks, and disappeared.

Only in San Francisco

An antique cable car with its "dummy" (a kind of caboose) becomes a coffee bar at Hallidie Plaza.

And then there are the stories that could only happen here, the kinds of things that make tourists goggle, and make locals grin slightly and say: Welcome to San Francisco.

Everyone who comes here wants to ride the cable cars. That includes celebrities and visiting dignitaries, of whom San Francisco has a good many more than its fair share.

He was a very famous celebrity. He got on Ira's cable car at the Wharf, accompanied by a film crew intent on getting footage of the Great Star in San Francisco. The Great Star rode on the running board, smiling into the camera, hair blowing in the breeze.

Ira isn't exactly a cowboy, but he does

enjoy speed. So when the cable car turns toward Nob Hill and begins the steep descent down Washington, Ira opens it up. At Jones Street, the cable car plunges down the steepest grade of the line. Behind him, Ira hears someone yelling: "Cut! Cut!" He turns around, but all he sees is his conductor convulsed with laughter. The cable car reaches Taylor, barely slows for the intersection, and zooms downward toward Mason Street.

Downhill from Taylor on Washington Street, with the cable car barn on the right.

At the bottom of this hill, at Mason and Washington, is the cable car barn. And on this evening, there is a small group of people clustered on the corner. Muni big shots, in expensive suits, are in attendance for a safety presentation.

Ira pulls his cable car to a stop with a flourish as the Muni suits stare. Some of them look grim and angry; others are snickering. Only then does Ira turn to see what they're looking at.

Standing on the running board is the Famous Star, with his toupee flopped forward over his eyes.

"I was in trouble on that for seven years," Ira recalls, "because they said we were going too fast."

🚋 🚋 🚋

Horace was working the Hyde line when the inspector sent him out empty.

"How come?" he asked.

"Never mind." The inspector was uncharacteristically close-mouthed. "Just take it down to Geary, stop the car at the intersection and wait."

Horace shrugged and complied. At Geary, he noted the barricades, the mobs, the battalions of police blanketing Union Square. And there, on a flatbed truck across from the St. Francis Hotel, was presidential candidate Bill Clinton.

He didn't have time to notice much else, because as he pulled to a stop half a dozen hard-eyed men in suits jumped aboard. One of them flashed a Secret Service ID; the others fanned out through the car, waving

1 9

metal-detector wands and inspecting every compartment and every inch of the cable car. Then they came to the black gym bag in front of the grip.

Most gripmen keep such a bag on the car, to hold extra clothing, lunch, or other personal belongings. "That's my stuff," Horace told the Secret Service agent.

Short digression: Jammed cable cars are catnip to pickpockets. Every gripman has spotted one occasionally working the crowds in the compartment. When possible, the gripman may grab the offender and restrain him until the police arrive. (Yes, it's relevant; wait for it.)

The agent picked up Horace's bag, unzipped it, and unceremoniously began yanking things out of it.

"Hey!" Horace said.

The agent ignored him. He pulled each item from the bag, examined it without expression, and tossed it onto the dirty floor of the cable car — a clean shirt, an apple, Horace's checkbook.

Suddenly, Horace remembered what else he had in the bag.

The agent reached inside and pulled out a pack of condoms, which he examined with the same lack of expression. Horace winced. And finally, the agent reached into the bag one more time and withdrew — a pair of handcuffs.

Horace felt his face redden. The agent's eyes flicked over him, but his stony face remained immobile as he completed his search of the bag, tossed everything back inside, and finally motioned to candidate Clinton to come on board.

In all the many encounters between cable cars and Secret Service agents, there is only one recorded instance of an agent cracking a smile.

Secretary of State Madeline Albright was staying at the Fairmont, so of course the area around California and Powell was stiff with security. Dana, gripping a Cal car toward the Embarcadero, had just crossed Powell and was heading downhill when the Highway Patrol car pulled alongside.

"Can we go around you?" the patrolman called out the window.

"Nope." Dana shook his head, with a big grin on his face to show he was teasing. He eased up on the grip slightly to increase his downhill speed, bringing him alongside a big black Chevy Suburban, with darkly-tinted windows.

With an audible bzzz, the tinted window slid down, and a pretty blonde woman looked out at Dana. She didn't say a word; instead, her lips turned up in a slight smile as she gently patted the Uzi poking above the door frame.

"I never hit a brake that fast in my life," Dana says.

The next time you complain that the cable cars are delayed, remember — this is San Francisco.

The milling hordes wandering the intersection at Hyde and Lombard.

Lombard Street, from Hyde down to Leavenworth, is billed by the Visitors Bureau as "the crookedest street in the world." It isn't, of course; in fact, it's not even the crookedest street in San Francisco. Still, tourists love it, and there are always clusters of people milling around at Hyde and Lombard, annoying locals and getting in the way of the cable cars.

That's why Matt didn't notice the guy on skis until he'd stopped at the intersection.

Skis? Matt looked more closely. Skis; only, these had little wheels attached to them.

The guy was positioned right next to the Hyde Street cable car tracks, facing down the long, steep hill toward Chestnut Street. Matt, looking down the hill to Chestnut, spotted a big wooden structure with a curl at the end, like a skateboard ramp.

He made the connection a moment too late, just as the guy on skis hurled himself over the crest and plummeted down the hill.

The Lombard-to-Chestnut run isn't the steepest hill on the line, but it is the longest, and by the time the guy reached the ramp he'd worked up a serious head of steam.

"He hit that thing dead on," Matt recalls, shaking his head. "He went up, did a mid-air flip, came down, and boom! just hit the ground like a rock, right in the middle of the street."

The cable car line was stopped for nearly an hour until paramedics and police cleared the scene.

It's not every day you see a gripman riding up the hill with his running board under his arm.

Picture it — a drizzly Wednesday morning at California and Drumm. Two cable cars are sitting in the layover area on California; Derek's car is across Drumm next to the Hyatt Regency, waiting to pull out.

Suddenly two men burst out into the street. One of them is wearing elaborate, if badly-applied, makeup — face powder, bright red blusher, eye shadow, mascara. He's waving a small object high over his head, which on close examination turns out to be a small disposable cigarette lighter.

The other man chases him out into the middle of California Street. The man in makeup, screaming and flapping his arms, takes evasive maneuvers, running a zigzag pattern back and forth across the cable car tracks. He runs a circle around the cable cars; the second man, also screaming, is in hot pursuit, a couple of steps behind.

Even for San Francisco, this is street theater of a pretty high order. Office-bound workers stop to goggle and giggle; people peer out of shop doors to watch; and on the cable cars, gripmen and conductors are craning their necks, convulsed with laughter.

"Oh, it was straight out of a comic book." Denny giggles at the memory. "I'm telling you, I'd have worked free that day just to see it."

The two men chase each other some more. Finally, inevitably, the man in makeup trips and falls, in the middle of the street, directly in front of the line of cable cars. Instantly, the second man is on him.

"Help me! Somebody help me!" The man in makeup is on his back, screaming and clutching the cigarette lighter. The second man is holding him down and trying ineffectually to grab the lighter out of his hand.

Up and down the street, everyone is transfixed by the flailing duo. That includes Derek, who's about to pull his cable car out of the plaza and across Drumm.

Enter the woman in the brand-new Camaro.

She drives down California, goggles at the spectacle, and stops for the red light at Drumm. She goggles some more. With her attention divided, she senses rather than sees the traffic light change. She swings her car into a left turn.

And rams her Camaro right into the side of Derek's oncoming cable car, shattering the cable car's (luckily empty) running board.

By the time the police arrive, the two men are no longer rolling around in the street; now they're standing at the curb jawing at each other. The police take statements from a sheepish Derek; from the apologetic driver of the Camaro; from hysterically laughing bystanders.

"Those two idiots are the ones you ought to arrest," Denny tells the cop. "Out there in the middle of the street like that fighting over a cheap cigarette lighter."

The cop looks at the two men. He looks at Denny. Then he bursts out laughing, shakes his head, gets back in his patrol car and drives away.

And that's why Derek was gripping his cable car up the hill with his running board under his arm.

Normally, passengers wearing backpacks are told to remove them before boarding, especially if they're standing out on the running board. Occasionally, the gripman doesn't warn them in time.

It was a foggy, foggy night on Nob Hill. As Terrell's cable car began its turn off Powell onto Jackson, a man appeared out of the fog. He ran for the car, grabbed the rail, and swung himself aboard. The cable car swung into the turn, closely clearing a truck parked on the corner.

Terrell noticed the man's backpack an instant too late — just before it caught on the truck's side-view mirror. Before Terrell could stop the cable car, man and truck disappeared behind it into the fog.

If San Francisco is the multicultural face of the new America, the cable cars are one of its most visible examples. Gripmen come in more flavors than Ben and Jerry's — and if that's a borderline ethnic joke, it's right at home here, where gripmen of every imaginable ethnic group positively relish the politically incorrect punch line.

No one in contemporary America is truly color-blind, and cable car operators don't pretend to be. What they are, instead, is perhaps the most comfortably race-conscious milieu imaginable.

There is a group of operators who fly to Texas every year for a week-long fishing trip — two African American, one Latino, one Anglo, one Chinese

American. One of the things they relish most is the look on the faces of the good old boys at the boat rental when this polymorphous group shows up.

And then there are the ethnic jokes.

Union Square, at Powell and Geary, is historically the prime spot for street theater in San Francisco. Magicians, mimes, and organ grinders have performed there over the years, some of them, like the mime duo of Shields and Yarnell, even going on to professional careers.

Recently, the corner has been the location for "living statues." Two or three men, painted from head to toe in metallic gold, silver, or bronze, will often pose there in a surprisingly effective display.

Gripmen have taken to calling them "the colored guys."

Lem (who is African American) was approaching the corner one afternoon when a tourist asked him for directions to Nieman-Marcus.

"It's just on the next corner." He pointed. "Right past the colored guys."

The car full of tourists looked shocked, and Rico heard one of them mumble: "I thought San Francisco was supposed to be such a politically correct city."

🚋 🚋 🚋

Gar (who is African American) had just pulled his car to the end of the Cal line at Van Ness. A pair of friendly tourists from Minnesota were making the round trip, but they asked Gar if they'd have time to get off and take a couple of pictures.

"Sure." Gar stepped down off the car and headed for the other end, but the tourists stopped him.

"Would you be in the picture too?" the man asked.

"Oh yes, please," the woman said. "We really want some local color." Only when Gar burst out laughing did they realize what they'd said.

Nor are they terribly impressed with cultural hypersensitivity.

Miles (who is African American) stopped his cable car in front of the St. Francis hotel one evening, and an Asian tourist got off.

For some reason Miles thought he was Japanese. "Sayonara," he said to him politely.

The tourist went ballistic.

"Do not say that to me," the man shouted. "I am not Japanese." He all but spat out the word. "I am Korean."

"Sorry." Miles shrugged.

"Sorry." The man refused to be mollified. "You insult me and that's all you can say?"

"Okay." Miles stared down at the man with contempt for his irrational temper. "I'm sorry I thought you were Japanese. But you know you guys all look alike."

> "Sometimes I'll say something in Japanese to a Japanese person, and they'll just look at me. And I'll say: do you speak Japanese? And they'll say, yeah. Then I'll say the word again. And they go, Ohh! Because they're not expecting that word to come out of my mouth."

You stereotype these guys at your peril. There's an Anglo gripman who speaks Japanese. There's a Latino who speaks German, courtesy of a tour of duty with the U.S. Army. One African American gripman speaks Hindi, and another speaks Chinese.

"It's funny to watch the tourists react," Whit says. "I'll get into a conversation with a Chinese passenger, and the tourists are looking at me like: Is he really speaking Chinese, or is it just gibberish and he's putting us on?" He shakes his head. "They just can't believe a black man would be speaking Chinese."

In fact, sometimes even native speakers don't recognize their own language if they're not expecting it.

Rico (who is Anglo) heard the man speaking Japanese, so he said a few words to him in the same language. The man just stared at him.

"Don't you speak Japanese?" Rico asked him in English.

"Yes, of course," the man replied.

Rico had to repeat the words twice before the light dawned.

🚋 🚋 🚋

Harley (who is African American) learned to speak Hindi from a woman he'd dated, so when the Indian couple boarded his cable car, he greeted them in that language.

The man looked at him blankly and shook his head. Harley repeated the greeting.

"I'm sorry." The man shook his head. "I do not understand what you are saying."

Harley repeated the words once more, enunciating carefully. Still the man looked blank.

Finally his wife, laughing, poked him with her elbow. "Dummy," she said. "He's not speaking English, he's speaking Hindi."

"We Don't Do Curb Service"

They're open on both sides. They stop in the middle of the street. There are signs at every corner along every line indicating where to wait.

So how come people have so much trouble getting on and off cable cars?

Even the most experienced locals will admit that correct boarding procedure can be violently non-intuitive, mostly because of the peculiar physics of cable cars. Depending on the steepness of the grade and the pattern of traffic, cars may stop before the intersection, across the intersection, or even in the middle of the intersection. And regardless of signage, confused tourists routinely try to climb aboard in the wrong place.

For instance: At California and Powell, all Cal cars stop on the west side of Powell, and all Powell cars stop on the north side of California. Yet it's a common sight to see tourists clustered on the wrong side of the intersection, frantically chasing a car across the street as it sweeps past them over the crest.

You'd think that boarding procedures would at least be obvious at the terminus of each line. You'd be wrong.

You'd be wrong especially at the end of the Cal line.

Here's the way it works:

Eastbound cable cars, coming from Van Ness, pull to a stop at Drumm Street, the end of the California line. There, they wait in a row, *still on the eastbound track,* until it's time for their next trip.

There is no turntable on the Cal line, because these double-ended cars operate in either direction. So when the next car is ready to leave, it pulls across Drumm into the little plaza next to the Hyatt Regency Hotel and the conductor pulls a handle which switches the track to outbound (westbound) mode.

Enter the average tourist, who sees a line of cable cars with no "front" or "back," and doesn't notice that they're on the eastbound track. Quite sensibly, the tourist assumes that the car at the westbound end of the line is the next westbound car.

On occasion, when nobody spots them in time, several dozen people will arrange themselves happily throughout the car. They're a lot less happy when they see the next westbound cable car sweep past them.

Usually, of course, an operator will stop them as they're climbing aboard. The following conversation is typical:

Tourist: "How soon do you leave?"
Operator (pointing across Drumm): "We're not the next car, ma'am. You board across the street at the plaza."
Tourist (peering roughly eastward): "Where?"
Operator (patiently): "Across the street next to the hotel."
Tourist (pointing toward an office building along California): "There?"
Operator (pointing firmly across Drumm): "No, ma'am, over there. At the end of the tracks. Just follow the tracks."
Tourist: "Oh, okay." They'll nod and get off the car; then, maybe one out of ten times, off they trot in the wrong direction. In another one out of the ten, the little group will "follow the tracks" in absolutely literal fashion, walking directly *on* the tracks right down the middle of California Street, totally oblivious to the cars and trucks roaring by.

There are also, incomprehensibly, numerous cases of tourists boarding a car in the *middle* of the row of waiting cars, and asking the gripman if this is the next car leaving. For these people, there is no hope.

There are one or two corners where boarding is not permitted, usually in the block directly past the turntables. Sometimes, tourists who think they're being clever try to board here rather than stand in the interminable lines.

One of these corners is at Ellis, where the Powell cars pass as they leave the Market Street turntable heading toward Fisherman's Wharf. Notwithstanding the sign that reads "Do Not Board Here," every gripman has had to turn people away at Ellis. Most of these would-be passengers grumble but step down. Some of them don't.

Ned's car is stopped for the red light at Ellis when the man climbs aboard.

"You can't board here," Ned tells him.

The guy ignores him.

"Step down, please," Ned says firmly.

The guy steps forward instead. "Shut up and drive," he snarls. Then he slaps Ned across the face, hard.

Ned is young, and recently ex-Navy. "The next thing I remember," he says, "we're on the ground and I've got my knee across his throat."

After a couple of hearings in which he described the incident, he wound up with a 3-day suspension. "And that was only because I was off the car."

The signage at Market and Ellis is pretty clean -- which doesn't necessarily mean people pay it any attention.

Figuring out how and where to board a cable car is the first problem. For some tourists, even figuring out which cable car to board, and in which direction, can be a problem.

Cable Car Confidential

If you look at a map — something too many tourists never bother to do — you'll see that the California cable car line does not go to Fisherman's Wharf. For locals, this is one of its advantages; for tourists, it is often a source of intense confusion.

If you're on California Street, and you want to go to the Wharf by cable car, you take a Cal car up to the top of Nob Hill, and you change to one of the other lines at Powell Street. Not hideously complicated — in fact, the only thing you really have to know is which way is up.

Yet it happens at least two or three times every weekend. A California cable car, heading east — downhill — *away* from Powell — rolls to a stop at Sansome, four blocks from the end of the line. And a group of tourists clambers aboard.

What happens next depends on the whim of the gripman. And because most gripmen are good guys, generally they'll ask: "Where do you people want to go?"

The answer, of course, is nearly always: "Fisherman's Wharf."

In fact, the California line in general seems to confuse tourists. They've internalized the equation "cable cars=Fisherman's Wharf;" nobody ever told them about the Cal line.

"Where does this go?"
"Where do you want to go?"
"We don't care."
"Then why are you asking?"

Except they're awfully disappointed when they get to Van Ness Avenue, an ugly corner with no tourist charm whatsoever.

Even on one of the Powell lines, which really do go to the wharf, that equation occasionally gets them into trouble. Because "Fisherman's Wharf" isn't a single, coherent destination. What it is, is nine blocks of schlock extending along Jefferson and Beach Streets, from Ghirardelli Square at one end to Pier 39 at the other. Along its length are mediocre-to-awful restaurants, wax museums, mediocre-to-awful art galleries, more restaurants, and hundreds of shops selling every conceivable artifact on which an image of a cable car can possibly be imprinted. In a city with some of the best shopping and best food in the world, Fisherman's Wharf is a nine-block monument to bad taste and bad cooking.

Problems arise because there are two different cable car lines to the Fisherman's Wharf area. One of them — the Hyde Street line — takes the scenic route over Russian Hill, ending in a descent of breathtaking views that even locals

3 0

The (totally non-scenic) turntable at Bay and Taylor.

never grow too blasé to appreciate. The Hyde line ends at Aquatic Park just behind Ghirardelli Square, facing a gorgeous sweep of bay and bridge.

The Bay-Taylor line, on the other hand, is short, relatively flat, and has virtually no scenic qualities whatsoever. It ends three blocks from the bay, at the edge of an ugly public housing project.

Unfortunately, it's the Bay-Taylor line that ends nearest to Pier 39, a destination incomprehensibly dear to most tourists. Spectacular views, or Bugs Bunny t-shirts — you pay your money and you take your choice.

For reference, you tell the two lines apart by color. The signs on the Hyde line cars, front, rear, and rooftop, are maroon; those on the Bay-Taylor cars are yellow.

And then there are your basic unclear-on-the-concept problems:

Tourist (on a stopped cable car): "Can we get off here?"
Gripman (grinning): "I don't know. Are your legs working?"

Tourist: "Is this where we get off?"
Gripman: "Where do you want to go?"
Tourist: "Here."

Tourist (a believer in the zoo-train theory): "Does it circle around and come back?"

Even when they're at the right place at the right intersection, tourists will often remain at the curb, milling in confusion, when a cable car pulls to a stop. To which the usual gripman's call is: "Let's go, folks. We don't do curb service."

And sometimes, things get just plain weird.

The guy didn't look drunk, but Linc figures he had to be, because he can't come up with any other plausible explanation.

He was an ordinary man in an ordinary business suit, and he approached the cable car and stepped onto the running board. Then he stepped up onto the landing in front of the bench. Then he stepped up onto the bench itself.

And then, as Linc stared in disbelief, he stepped up onto the back of the bench and was just about to launch himself into the grip hole when Linc grabbed him and ushered him firmly off the car.

Dangerous Maneuvers

Because cable cars run down the middle of the street, passengers getting on or off must make their way across at least one lane of traffic. This is bad enough at traditional corners. But on steep hills, cable cars have to stop on the flat surface directly in the middle of the intersection. At these points The City's traffic department, in its infinite wisdom, has chosen to have the lights remain green in the cable car's direction, so that people getting on and off must cross against the light. On a good day, you're looking at an advanced game of Passenger Pinball.

For situations exactly like this, there is California Vehicle Code 21756(a), which reads:

> The driver of a vehicle overtaking any interurban electric or streetcar stopped or about to stop for the purpose of receiving or discharging any passenger shall stop the vehicle to the rear of the nearest running board or door of such car and thereupon remain standing until all passengers have boarded the car or upon alighting have reached a place of safety. . . . may proceed past such car at a speed not greater than 10 miles per hour and with due caution for the safety of pedestrians.

In other words, drivers are required to yield to boarding and disembarking

A cable car stops, correctly, in the middle of the California-Hyde intersection.

passengers. And if you believe that San Francisco drivers will stop politely behind a cable car, you also believe in deregulated electricity and the tooth fairy.

Cable car operators, who understand the hazard, constantly warn passengers to watch for traffic. Some conductors carry whistles to use against passing cars. At particularly dangerous intersections, some will step off the car (a strict violation of Muni regs) and escort passengers to the curb. All of them are angered by drivers who risk lives by ignoring the law.

And then there's Jake.

For Jake, this is a personal vendetta. Jake will leap out in front of a speeding car, screaming and waving his arms. Jake will personally escort people to the curb. And when even that doesn't work, well...

California at Hyde Street is one of those middle-of-the-intersection stops. And at 7:30 in the morning, drivers racing to their jobs in the Financial District don't want to hear about California Vehicle Code 21756(a).

At that hour, most of the passengers are regulars. So was the handicapped woman who maneuvered herself off the car at Hyde in the middle of roaring traffic and headed across the street on her crutches.

Jake — of course — jumped off the cable car, took her by the elbow, and held out his hand to stop traffic. As Jake tells it, "this guy drives up, and his car hits my hand with one of those spring-loaded Jeep mirrors."

A fairly minor incident — for anyone but Jake.

The Jeep driver says a few words. Jake says a few words. Some of the regular passengers say a few words to the driver.

"You trying to kill someone?" One of the regulars, carrying a cane himself, yells at the driver. "You're supposed to stop for cable cars." There are shouts of agreement from other passengers. Jake adds his own pithy comments.

The driver of the Jeep is young and expensively dressed and on his way to a Very Important Job. He isn't about to take this from someone who rides public transportation. He damn sure isn't about to take it from someone who *drives* public transportation. Some more words are exchanged, and the driver opens the door of his Jeep and starts to get out.

The passenger with the cane looks at the young guy in his snappy business suit. He looks at Jake, all 6'2", 220 pounds of him. He reaches out with his cane and shoves the Jeep's door shut. "Uh-uh." He shakes his head at the driver. "You're too young to die."

The driver looks at Jake, does a little more yelling and screaming from the safety of his Jeep, and finally drives away. But when the cable car reaches Mason Street, there's the Jeep once more.

"Hey!" he yells out to the passengers on the running board. "You saw what happened, didn't you? You saw what he did to my car?"

"Yeah, we saw what happened," a passenger replies angrily. "We saw you nearly kill people."

The driver does a little more woofing, and finally drives off. Jake shrugs it off and finishes his run, pulling into line at California and Drumm.

And here comes the Jeep yet again. This time it pulls up alongside the cable car, and this time the driver jumps out of his car and storms toward Jake.

This time, with no passengers to be concerned about, Jake jumps to his feet in fury. He's fed up with this guy, and he's also not sure what he's got in mind. Maybe he's got a gun. Maybe he's looking for a fight.

"All right, you stupid son of a bitch, you gonna stop me, do it now." Jake is a believer in the best-defense-is-a-good-offense theory. He wiggles his fingers in a come-here motion. "You wanna do it? Let's do it."

The driver slows his approach.

"Come on," Jake shouts. "Pull your piece and get it over with." His eyes are bulging with rage. Jake is a big man; now, looming off the cable

*A Powell car stops to pick up the cable across California,
where jumping on or off is not only forbidden but dead stupid.*

car, he looks even bigger. "Come on, dickhead," he screams, "if you're
gonna shoot me, shoot me!"

The driver stops, and, in Jake's words, "looks at me kind of funny."
Suddenly, the driver seems to recall a Very Important Appointment. He
takes a step backward and mutters. He hops back into the Jeep. And he
rapidly drives away.

Jumping on or off a moving cable car is dangerous, dumb, and strictly prohibited. Yet people try it all the time. Nor are tourists the only perpetrators. Locals who should, and often do, know better still do the same.

For this, gripmen insist, Hollywood has much to answer for. In movies, on
television, and in commercials, people are shown gaily hopping on and off moving cable cars. But, as one gripman points out, those are stunt people performing
a maneuver that has been carefully choreographed and rehearsed.

Jumping onto a moving cable car is tricky enough. Jumping *off* is flat-out
stupid, about on par with a backflip off a balance beam on top of a trampoline.

At the corner of California and Powell, inbound Powell cars slow down to
pick up the cable before starting downhill. People who try to board at this point
are generally waved away by the gripman. But there isn't much they can do for
the idiots who decide to hop *off* just as the car starts moving. Every gripman can

regale you with stories about someone who jumped off, hit the ground like a human bowling ball, and rolled halfway down the hill.

And then there was the woman — no tourist, either, but a business-suited local — who committed an act of folly so astounding that gripmen who hear about it shake their heads in total disbelief.

She was on the running board of a Cal car heading downtown. Standing easily, high heels planted, briefcase in hand, she watched as an outbound cable car approached. And as the two cars passed, both of them going pretty close to a full nine and a half miles an hour, she jumped the gap from one car to the other.

Nine and a half miles an hour doesn't sound like much. But when you factor in issues of momentum and force, it increases exponentially. One gripman, hearing the story open-mouthed, estimated that if you jumped straight across, your landing would approximate hitting a wall at ninety miles an hour. "It is," he opined, "a good way to commit suicide."

In fact, a few years ago, while filming the movie "The Net" in San Francisco, the director asked for exactly this maneuver. On a closed street, with carefully-choreographed movements and split-second timing, a highly trained stunt woman jumped from one cable car to another cable car passing in the opposite direction.

The pole hit her in the face and broke her cheekbone.

The woman in the business suit was luckier. Instead of her jump taking her straight across the gap, it took her backwards from the momentum of the cable car she was on, cutting the force of her landing. Instead of hitting the pole, she hit a sitting passenger, landing against him with enough force to drive the air out of his lungs.

Instead of a shout of outrage, the only sound he could make was a gargled "oof."

A Few Tips

Okay, here's the stuff that's worth the price of the book — how savvy locals beat the system, and how you can, too.

Luckily for the locals, most tourists, bless their hearts, queue up politely at the obvious boarding spots. The lines at the turntables, for instance, aka the Yahoo Lines. Or the traffic island at Powell and Post, better known as Fantasy Island (it being pure fantasy that there'll be room on the cable car by the time it gets there.)

Locals will never tell, but there are methods, and locations, that can vastly increase your chances of getting on a cable car.

First of all, read the signs. Yes, the signs.

Muni has posted, at semi-vast expense, small brown-and-white signs at each intersection served by a cable car. Oddly enough, these signs actually provide several pieces of useful information.

First, they'll tell you if a cable car actually stops at the intersection. If the sign reads: "Do not board here," believe it; the gripman absolutely will not let you on.

Second, the sign will tell you which line or lines serve the intersection.

And finally, the sign will tell you where the cable car will stop. If you're standing on a corner and the small brown sign is across the street, you're in the wrong place. And if the sign reads "Car stops at mid-intersection," it means just that. Don't panic if it drives past your corner; it's simply pulling forward into the middle of the intersection.

An even simpler way to tell where a cable car will stop is to look for the broad yellow line painted on the pavement, right across the tracks; that's its stopping point. If the line is accompanied by a pair of X's, that means the cable car is officially required to make a stop even if no one is getting on or off; be aware, though, that gripmen, like other San Francisco drivers, are occasionally guilty of the California Stop, and at some double-X's, if they don't see you, they may sweep right on by.

Still, even being in the right place won't do you any good if the cable cars are full, which the two Powell lines almost always are during the tourist season. And in San Francisco, the tourist season is defined as any day with a "y" in it.

Here are a few tricks that experienced locals use to maximize their chances:

Going Outbound from Downtown:

You'll never see a local standing in the yahoo line at the Market Street turntable. Or on Fantasy Island. That's because they're two short blocks away, at O'Farrell, the best-kept secret of the Powell line. This is the first stop off the turntable, the one place where there's almost always room for a few people to squeeze on.

On Nob Hill:

Look for corners where people are most likely to get off. One of the best is Powell at Washington, where gripmen usually announce the stop for Chinatown. Chances are, at least a few people will get off, opening up space for newcomers.

Tourists cluster on Fantasy Island at Powell and Geary — file this under "never."

At Fisherman's Wharf:

There's no convenient O'Farrell-type stop at the Wharf. You can try Hyde at Northpoint, but a lot of gripmen won't stop there at all. If you must stand in line, go for the Bay-Taylor turntable, where the lines are a good bit shorter than those for the Hyde line at Aquatic Park. (And if you want to avoid standing in line entirely, go for the antique streetcars on the Muni F-line. They're beautiful, they run a scenic route along the Embarcadero, they only cost a buck, they give and take transfers, and they'll deposit you at Market and Powell just like the cable cars.)

For All Lines, Everywhere:

Wait on the *left* side of the street instead of on the right. Cable cars are open on both sides, remember? And since most people don't quite get it, there's always more likely to be a spot on the left side. So wait on the opposite curb; check the yellow line to see where the car will stop; then cross to it just as it rolls to a stop. If there's an opening on the running board, it's yours.

Of course, you'll have to cross a lane of traffic. But then, riding cable cars is always about no guts, no glory.

And one more thing. Gripmen being, well, gripmen, it also doesn't hurt to be female, young, pretty, and — more important than any of these — cheerful. (Blonde is an optional plus.)

The
Tower

Forget Market and Van Ness. Forget Broadway and 42nd Street. Forget the traffic circles of Rome. For seriously bad traffic craziness, you cannot do better than the corner of California and Powell.

This is where all three cable car lines cross at a steep crest atop Nob Hill, in a honking, rattling gavotte of terrified tourists and bewildered pedestrians and hulking tour buses and impatient cabs and oblivious delivery trucks.

On a good day, you could set up bleachers and sell tickets, just to watch the show.

It's easy for locals to laugh — or swear — at the insane bottleneck. But the truth is, this is a corner that is utterly incomprehensible on first sight.

At this one single intersection, there are the following <u>forty</u> signs or signals:

Eight standard street signs — on each corner, a large green sign and a smaller white sign identifying the cross street.

Eight sets of three-light traffic lights, two on each corner, each of them blinking red.

Eight smallish yellow signs reading: "Cross Street — Cable Cars Do Not Stop."

Four signs displaying a left-pointing arrow under a red circle and bar, the symbol for "No Left Turn."

Four brown-and-white cable car boarding signs.

Two brown-and-white cable car signs reading: "Do Not Board in This Area."

Two cable car traffic lights.

One sign posted below a cable car traffic signal reading: "Cable Car Signal Only."

Two large banners celebrating the 125th anniversary of the cable car.

One sign reading: "Commercial Vehicles Over 3 Tons Prohibited."

Is it any wonder that the average tourist drivers, unprepared for their first encounter with this sensory madhouse, will often simply freeze at the steering wheel?

Already unnerved by the steep hill, many of them will come over the crest, take one look at the intersection, and just stop dead, like a deer in the headlights. Out of the kaleidoscope of color and light and noise and bad signage, they cling to the only thing their overloaded senses recognize — the blinking red of a traffic light.

And so they sit, oblivious to the angry honking behind them, waiting for the flashing red light to turn green.

For cable cars, the only line of defense against this craziness is called the Tower.

"The Tower" is actually a tiny green-painted octagonal structure perched on the southeast corner of the intersection, wearing a conical pointed roof like a witch's hat. It is barely six feet in diameter and approximately twelve feet high, not counting the hat; like so much else about the cable cars, the Tower looks adorable — until you have to work in it.

Outbound on California, and outbound on Powell, the cable cars are heading steeply uphill. Because neither gripman can see over the crest, a signal system is needed. But because a cable car cannot stop once it starts uphill, a standard traffic light won't do.

Thus, the Tower, which in point of fact is nothing more — nor less — than a manually-operated traffic signal. An operator sits in the Tower, from which he can see the cable cars coming from all four directions, and switches the lights that signal each car when to start toward the intersection.

Cable Car Confidential

Cable cars crossing at California and Powell.

It's the easiest gig in cable car division, often assigned to guys recovering from injuries. Most of them loathe it.

Only Jake could cause a major incident while working there.

The story is neoclassic Jake, complete with hostile driver, physical danger, police confrontation, and protestations of total innocence.

There are, of course, some guys who don't mind working the tower, even though it's tiny, cramped, and not least, excruciatingly boring. Jake isn't one of those guys. Jake doesn't take well to boredom.

The tower operator usually directs cable car traffic from inside via the signal lights, but occasionally, in order to control vehicular traffic (or sometimes just for the physical freedom), he'll stand out in the intersection with a red traffic flag. It would come as no surprise to anyone who knows Jake that, on this rush-hour afternoon, he was outside with his flag, surrounded by racketing traffic.

A Powell Street car, at Jake's signal, was grinding its way uphill toward California from Pine Street. Another Powell car, going in the other direction, had just crossed California and paused at the lip of the hill for the take-rope. Jake stepped into the middle of the intersection, waving his flag to hold traffic until both cable cars cleared.

The Lexus, stopped behind the cable car at the take-rope, didn't want to be held. In fact, what the driver wanted was to turn left, which is illegal at any time, and just plain stupid with a cable car already in the intersection.

Ignoring Jake, the driver of the Lexus cut his wheel and started into his turn. Jake jumped in front of him, waving his flag frantically.

"Back up!" Jake yelled. "You're gonna get clobbered! There's a cable car coming!"

The driver of the Lexus didn't get it. Instead of backing up, he shook his head and waved Jake away. He was still shaking his head when he finally spotted the cable car cresting the hill, coming straight at him. With his wheels still aimed into the illegal left turn, he panicked and hit the accelerator.

And then ... well, let Jake tell it.

"See, his bumper was right at my knees. So when he shot forward, instead of having my knees snap out, what I did was I jumped up and onto the hood. And I grabbed hold of the edge of the wiper well in order to keep myself from being thrown off. I yelled at him: 'Stop, let me off! Let me off!' But the guy just kept on going.

"So now we're going down the hill on California toward Stockton, and he's swinging left and right, trying to shake me off the hood of his car. I'm hanging on to the wiper well with my fingers, and my legs are swinging back and forth in the air, and here we go careening down the hill like that."

Jake's eyes widen with the memory, and his face splits in a broad smile. "You could see all the operators up at Powell, looking down the hill with their mouths open, goggling at this whole thing."

By the time the motorcycle cop showed up, Jake was on his feet at Stockton, shaken but unhurt. Jake, of course, started jawing at the cop. "I said, this guy's obviously been drinking. You can freaking smell it. You don't take a guy downhill on the hood of your car trying to shake him off unless you're drunk."

The cop looked at Jake, furious and disheveled. He looked at the driver of the Lexus, in a business suit and an expensive car. Then he told Jake to go back up the hill to the tower and wait for him.

Jake climbed back up the hill and waited. By the time the cop rode his motorcycle up to join him, one of the suits from Muni had also arrived.

"The guy is drunk," Jake repeated.

The cop looked at the Muni suit, who shrugged his shoulders. "Well, this operator's just a little screwy," the suit said.

"He drove down the hill with me on his hood," Jake shouted. "He was trying to shake me off, trying to kill me."

"He thought you were some sort of crazy street person," the cop said.

"With my orange Muni vest on? Waving a red flag?" Jake screamed. "Are you nuts?"

Jake recounts the end of the story with satisfaction. "He went back down the hill and let the guy go, and I made a citizen's complaint to the police, and the cop got ten days' suspension."

Cable Car Confidential

*Just another near-collision
at California and Powell.*

If you look closely at the tower, you'll note that it's ringed by three-foot metal t-bars set in concrete. These are not for decoration, as Gavin can attest.

The story actually starts down in the Tenderloin, where a delivery company parks its trucks overnight. Some time during one particular night, someone happened to toss a newspaper toward one of the trucks. The newspaper happened to slip down between the cargo box and the cab, coming to rest against the manifold.

And the next morning, as the driver made his deliveries, the manifold began to heat up.

The driver, of course, knew nothing about the errant newspaper — until he was halfway up the Powell Street hill from Pine to California. That's when he saw a pedestrian on the sidewalk gesticulating wildly and shouting: "Hey! Your truck's on fire!"

The driver looked in his mirror, saw flames shooting out of his truck, and pulled over to the curb in a panic.

Unfortunately, he was already at the curb, directly next to the tower.

Gavin, meanwhile, was sitting in the tower minding his own business, which was of course to work the cable car traffic signals. He was looking the other way, down California, when he saw, out of the corner of his eye, a shadow looming behind him.

That was immediately before the Kaboom! that shook the tower to its foundation as the burning truck rammed the steel posts.

The Fairmont Hotel, on the northwest block of California and Powell, is one of the Grand Old Ladies among San Francisco hotels. As such, it's often the hotel of choice for visiting dignitaries, especially politicians during rutting season. And if the intersection is nightmarish at the best of times, a visiting president kicks up the pain factor to nearly indescribable.

Presidents — or presidential candidates, for that matter — do not travel as do ordinary mortals. They proceed in entourages, limos following limos, staff cars following staff cars, all of it surrounded by outriggers of police motorcycles and street barricades and traffic patrols and motley groups of sign-waving supporters, protesters, and the just plain wacked.

And finally, guarding the perimeter of this traveling circus, are more Secret Service agents than movies or television can possibly prepare you for.

The main entrance to the Fairmont is a block uphill on Mason Street, but presidents do not use main entrances. Instead, they are whisked in and out by limo through the hotel garage entrance on Powell Street. At these moments, all traffic for a block in each direction is cleared out of the way. This includes cable cars.

Two cable cars stopped for passengers at California and Powell Streets, in front of the Fairmont Hotel garage.

Roger, working the tower during one of these campaign visits, knew the presidential entourage would be leaving eventually, but he didn't know when. For the moment, he was simply directing cable car traffic in the ordinary way, waiting for orders to stop them.

A Hyde line cable car, coming up from the Wharf, had just pulled to a stop in the usual place, which is directly in front of the Fairmont's garage opening. A California line cable car, coming up from the Embarcadero, had just reached Stockton and was waiting for the signal to proceed uphill. Roger flicked the Powell signals red, and the Cal signal green. The Cal car started up the steep grade.

In front of the Fairmont garage, a Secret Service agent, armed, grim-faced, hard-eyed, received word through his earpiece to clear the street. Instantly and urgently, he ordered the Hyde line cable car to start moving. The young gripman, required by Muni regs to obey the orders of all appropriate police agencies, did as he was told.

"It was," Roger recalls, "the closest to disaster I've ever seen."

The Cal car was halfway up the hill when Roger realized the Hyde car was moving. He leaped out of the tower and raced into the intersection, frantically waving his arms in all directions. The Hyde car stopped; the Cal car managed to stop just over the crest; Roger took a deep breath.

"He told me to move." The young Hyde car gripman, shaken, jerked his head backward at the Secret Service agent.

Roger doesn't remember what he said. "I just went off on him like an M-One," he reports, grinning.

And for perhaps the only time on record, a Secret Service agent apologized to a civilian.

Sex and the Cable Cars

It can't be the uniforms. Screamingly ugly brown polyester is hardly young love's romantic dreams. So what is it about cable car gripmen that makes them babe magnets?

That they are, is of course nothing new. Cable car groupies are the stuff of legend. Everybody's heard the stories; everybody insists they happened to other people, in other times.

"Oh, that was back in the sixties and seventies," they insist, shaking their heads in sorrow at having been born too late. "Back then, pretty girls'd even bring their own blankets and pillows."

Even today, in these politically correct, post-feminist days, pretty girls still flock around them. So do middle-aged women, and happily married women, and elderly women, and high-profile, power-suited professional women.

Gripmen regularly have hotel keys slipped into their pockets; and sure, sometimes they'll follow up on the invitation. On the other hand, more often than you'd imagine, they are the object of not-so-subtle groping, by female tourists intoxicated by what they fondly believe is licentious San Francisco. Not surprisingly, gripmen are no more thrilled by this kind of assault than the average woman would be. And, just as much to the point, they find this kind of behavior distastefully... unladylike.

It doesn't hurt that so many of these guys are, to be blunt, babes themselves. But that's not really what it's about. Maybe the bottom line is simply that these guys like women. Like them, that is, in an old-fashioned, uncomplicated way that has nothing, and everything, to do with sexuality. And women, sensing that, return the compliment in the same uncomplicated fashion. They like these guys — like them as people, and as men. And something more — in some odd way, these guys feel *safe*.

Their attitudes toward women, in fact, are an odd mixture of old-fashioned virtues and old-fashioned vices — chivalry and severe judgmentalism, old-fashioned gallantry combined with modern expectations. Call it chivalry turned on its head, with a postmodern spin.

Most of them will stop dead in the middle of a conversation — or in the middle of the street — to ogle a good-looking woman. Yet many of them have stories of defending women from bullying men. They play at being rogues, yet they treat women with almost courtly grace. They treat them, in fact, like ladies — which is also how they expect them to behave. Old-fashioned virtues, old-fashioned vices.

At the same time, they work hard at being hounds. Conversation — and for that matter, operations — are always subject to interruption when a pretty woman walks by.

Josh is talking to a woman friend about the 49ers. The conversation is complex and esoteric, revolving around cornerback techniques and tight coverage. "If he plays off five yards," Josh says, "he isn't quick enough to..."

His voice dies away, and his eyes drift off into the middle distance. The woman he's talking to turns around, knowing what she'll see — pretty woman, tight skirt, clingy top, long legs in high heels.

"Any time you're finished..." the woman says amiably.

"Mm-mmmh." Josh returns her grin, unabashed. "Now that's nice."

He wouldn't, of course, even think of indulging in wolf whistles or catcalls, because this isn't about macho display. It's simply about appreciation.

Hyde Street at Beach, looking across toward the turntable at Aquatic Park.

Benjy's cable car was at the end of the Hyde line, in front of the Buena Vista. He was heading across Beach Street to the turntable, just as he'd done hundreds of times before. Only...

"There was a wonderful pair of white jeans." Even now, a slight smile crosses Benjy's face. "And I mean, it had my undivided attention, it really did."

The white jeans, clearly, were more compelling than the bumper bar, the underground metal barrier which protects the cable at those places where the grip is supposed to be released. Benjy, focused on those white jeans, forgot to release the grip.

The cable car slammed into the bumper bar at full grip. The impact hurled Benjy forward, straight down into the grip hole.

"My feet were all the way to the pavement," Benjy says, laughing, "Let me tell you, I came out of there a lot faster than I went in."

And of course, they'll cheerfully take what they can get — sometimes.

The apartment on Hyde Street near Beach overlooked the cable car waiting area, so of course the operators had a good view — and it was a very good view. The woman had been tantalizing them for weeks with a peep show that always seemed to stop just short of the big finish, but the operators kept watching, and hoping.

This day, it looked like their hopes might be fulfilled. As Lloyd and Jamal watched from their car, she paraded past the window, shedding clothing as she went.

Lloyd waved to the guys in the other cars; Jamal clanged on the bell to alert them; from the turntable, gripmen came racing across Beach. Halfway up the hill, Brad saw the action down below and shoved the grip forward, skinning the rope in his desperate flight.

The woman was down to lacy underwear. She turned her back, removed the last filmy shreds, and turned toward the window with a flourish.

She was a guy.

🚋 🚋 🚋

"Want a Life Saver?"

Gervase was on break at the end of the Cal line, half-asleep on his car. "No, thanks." He didn't bother to open his eyes.

"You sure? It's a pre-wedding dare." The voice was young and female, accompanied by a cascade of giggles. But he didn't bother to check it out, just shook his head.

"I'll take one." That was Monty; well, he'd never met a piece of candy he didn't like. Gervase dozed on. "Me, too." "Hey, count me in." Half a dozen gripmen and conductors chimed in, and now Gervase was starting to wonder. All that excitement for a couple of Life Savers? He popped his eyelids slightly to see what was going on. Then he opened them all the way and sat up straight.

Standing by the next car was a pretty blonde in a tight pink sweater, accompanied by two other young women. The blonde was the source of the Life Savers, all right. Only, instead of holding out the familiar multicolored roll, she had them sewn onto her sweater. And one by one, guys were invited to <u>bite</u> them off.

And Gervase suddenly had this craving for a Life Saver...

🚋 🚋 🚋

Omar was inbound on the Hyde line late one night when the woman made him the usual offer.

She wanted him, and she wanted him right away. And, in the manner of sloppy drunks, she wouldn't take no for an answer.

Omar was no saint, but he figured she was too drunk to know what she was doing. He also figured she was probably too drunk to make it home. So, near the top of the Hyde Street hill, he stopped the cable car, left his conductor to hold it, and helped the woman stagger the remaining two blocks to her apartment.

"I got her into her living room," Omar recalls, "and told her I'd take a

5 0

rain check until the next day." He shrugged. "Then I went back the two blocks to the cable car and took it on downtown."

He never said whether he cashed the rain check.

Sometimes, in fact, they'll carry the defense of women to extremes — as in:

The Case of the Kidnapped Wife

The conventioneers had spent the evening getting well oiled at Fisherman's Wharf. Now they were riding the Hyde line down to Market Street, shooting off their mouths and not worrying overmuch about who got caught in the crossfire.

Business as usual for a lot of conventioneers. Except, this time one of them had his wife along.

She was a pretty lady, with soft brown curls and a sweet expression that could easily be mistaken for weakness. And as the antics of her husband and his buddies got raunchier and raunchier, Tina was getting more and more upset.

"Hey, don't let them get to you." Denny was conducting, and he purely hated to see a pretty woman cry. "You know, sometimes guys'll be guys." He patted her on the shoulder. "You come on and stand back here with me."

Out of the drunken babble, her husband's voice floated back to them.

"Hey, who needs that shit?" he was saying loudly. "They ain't a woman alive worth that."

"You din't say that back that time in Houston, Charley." His companions whooped and slapped him on the back. "You thought that purty l'il secretary was just fine, din't he, fellas?"

"Oh, she was a real fine little ol' piece. Wish I coulda brought some o' that home with me." Charley's voice was slurred, but the words that drifted back to the conductor's platform were unfortunately crystal clear to his wife. Tina burst into tears.

Denny patted her on the back, wishing he could do something for her, and after a couple of minutes Tina stopped crying and started getting angry.

"Boy, I'd like to get back at them." She hiccupped. "I wish I could fix that son-of-a-bitch good."

"Well, now..." Denny was having an idea. He looked at Tina and grinned. She gave him a watery smile in return. "Okay," Denny said, "here's what we do. When we get to the end of the line at Market Street everyone has to get off the car. Now what we'll do is, you stay on the

Powell Street cable car begins the uphill run at Sutter.

car, we'll turn it around, and we'll grab the rope real quick and take off. We leave them there at the turntable, they're gonna think you're gone."

Tina cocked her head and thought about it and found it good. "Yeah, let's do it."

At Market Street, the merry conventioneers got off while Tina stayed on the back, and as soon as the car slid off the turntable they hit the rope and took off.

Up to O'Farrell the car went, and on to Geary. The conventioneers staggered along behind, laughing and whooping over this hilarious new game. Not until the cable car reached Post did reality finally penetrate their alcoholic haze.

"Hey!" The guys, now two blocks back, started trotting faster up Powell. "What's goin' on?"

"Keep going, keep going," Tina urged.

"Hey, you! Come back with my wife!" The conventioneers, all half dozen of them, broke into a shambling run.

"Don't let them catch up!" Tina cried as the cable car reached Sutter. "Keep going!"

Denny looked at her. She had a big smile on her face, the first time she'd smiled since she'd gotten on the car. "Are you sure?"

"Damn right I am."

"Well, what the hell." Denny grinned widely, reached for the bell rope, and gave it two sharp yanks. The cable car began to climb.

From Market Street to Sutter, Powell is only a slight uphill grade, of the kind that half a dozen drunken good ol' boys can manage with only some heavy puffing. But at Sutter, Powell shoots upward like a roller coaster. Denny and Tina stood on the back platform, laughing and waving, as the posse fell further and further behind until they disappeared into the fog.

Denny and Tina talked and laughed some more as the cable car whined its way home to the barn. They were hitting it off pretty good, they realized; they were having fun; and when they got to the barn, they decided to keep the fun rolling for a while longer. Denny turned in his fares, and he and Tina split.

Give the conventioneers credit — they didn't quit. Half an hour later they staggered into the barn, panting and exhausted and a lot more sober than when they'd started.

"Where is she?" the husband demanded of the dispatcher.

"Where's who?"

"My wife! Your guy kidnapped my wife!"

There were a couple of other gripmen sitting around, and they started snickering. This was a joke, right?

"It's no joke!" the husband screamed. "You call the police right now!" Which the dispatcher, having no choice, shrugged and proceeded to do.

And Denny and Tina? They spent the weekend in Sausalito, maxing out Tina's husband's credit cards and having the time of their lives. Not until a week later did Denny find out that, for a couple of days, he'd been a fugitive from the FBI.

Members of the Club

It isn't exactly the Mile-High Club, but it has a certain similar appeal. Call it the Nine-and-a-Half-Mile-an-Hour Club. And an awful lot of people want to become members.

It was nearly midnight on the Hyde Line, heading outbound toward Fisherman's Wharf. Lydia was conducting, standing on the back deck of a nearly-deserted car, looking forward into the compartment where the only two passengers were sitting.

They weren't taking up much space, either, because the woman was sitting on the man's lap, her legs straddling his. And from the way they were rocking back and forth, Lydia was pretty sure they weren't there to watch the scenery go by.

They weren't very good at it, either. When the cable car finally crested the hill at Lombard, they were still working at it, and Lydia was fed up with watching them. The gripman, of course, faced forward, so Lydia had the show all to herself. Finally she opened the compartment door and stuck her head inside.

"Okay, knock it off," she said. "You guys are gonna have to take it somewhere else."

"Hey, that's okay." The guy winked at Lydia, his ferretty face flushed. He didn't stop what he was doing. "C'mon in," he invited. "You can get in on it too."

Proving, as Lydia put it, that there are some offers you can refuse.

Nudes Descending

As near as anyone can tell, there's just something about cable cars that makes people want to get naked. There must be. How else can you explain the startling number of escapades over the years?

"There was just something about her," Dexter's hindsight recalls. "Like she was acting weird, you know?"

She got on at Bay Street, pretty but not gorgeous, just another blonde in a trench coat hanging onto the pole at the front of the car, and after a quick look, Dexter didn't pay any attention to her. That is, until the cable car reached Chestnut Street.

That's when he noticed the cameras a little way up the hill. That's also when the woman removed her trench coat, leaned out from the running board, and posed seductively for the cameras.

She was, of course, stark naked.

🚋 🚋 🚋

"Mind if I take a few pictures?" the man asked.

"Sure, no problem." Grant, the conductor, shrugged easily.

"This is Dolores." The man indicated a pretty woman in a fur coat. "She's a model. We'd like to set her up at the front stanchion, then we'll drive ahead of the cable car and photograph her going up the hill, okay?"

"Sure," Grant said again. He watched the woman position herself, her back to him, then forgot her as he went about collecting fares.

Only, as the cable car started up the hill from Kearny, he noticed the woman spreading her arms, flinging the fur coat open. Curious, he leaned around from the opposite side to see what she was wearing under the coat.

Absolutely nothing.

🚋 🚋 🚋

The pretty young woman was showing her mother the sights of San Francisco, pointing out landmarks and chatting with Randy in friendly fashion. As they started down the Hyde Street hill, Randy commented on the elaborate pendant she wore around her neck.

"That's real nice," he said. "What does the design mean?"

"I don't know." She looked down at the pendant. "But I have the same design tattooed on my tailbone."

And as her mother beamed proudly, she stood up, dropped her pants, and leaned over to display her decorated rear end.

🚋 🚋 🚋

Gervase was running on the Hyde line, and he stepped into the BV for some coffee. "Well, it figures it would be the BV," he says.

The BV — the Buena Vista bar and restaurant — has always had a special relationship with the Hyde line gripmen. Back in the Good Old Days, the BV was where you went for a quick snort between runs, or where you warmed up over a couple of beers before heading back up the hill. Nowadays, of course...

So Gervase got his coffee and was turning to leave when a thirtyish tourist couple motioned to him.

"Has anyone ever ... you know, done it on a cable car?" the man asked. Gervase just laughed. "No, really." The guy pulled a wad of bills halfway out of his pocket and glanced from the money to Gervase meaningfully. "Any chance you'd be interested?" His pretty wife blinked her eyes at Gervase, looking eager.

Gervase is a good-looking guy, and it wasn't the first such offer he'd ever fielded. He looked at the man, and then looked at the wife, and then regretfully shook his head. "Sorry, guess not."

"Ah, come on," the man pressed. "You look like a guy who's up for some fun — if you know what I mean." The woman favored him with a big smile.

"Thanks, but I'll pass," Gervase said. "I have a lady of my own, and she wouldn't take kindly to it. If you know what I mean."

"Oh, that's not what I meant." The man shook his head. "I'm talking about the two of us." His face lit up. "But you can watch," he offered.

Gervase laughed aloud. "Hell, in that case, I'm definitely not interested."

And then there are inspectors.

The girl was selling ... well, let's just say she was selling. Anyway, the inspector — all 250 pounds of him — thought the price was right. He jerked his head toward the bathroom at the Bay-Taylor terminal, and the girl followed him inside.

Two minutes later, the gripmen lounging around their cable cars heard a crash, followed by muffled shouts, followed by the inspector hastily exiting from the bathroom with his trousers around his ankles.

It seems that, in order to expedite the experience, the inspector had levered his bulk onto the bathroom sink — which promptly collapsed under him.

And, this being San Francisco, sometimes cable car people just see more than they're intended to see.

The cable car is stopped for a red light at Mason and Jackson; so is the Beamer next to them. It's late at night, and Mona is conducting, standing at the rear brake waiting for the light to change. From her position on the back deck high above the street, she glances idly down into the Beemer.

The youngish guy in the driver's seat is stark naked.

Mona does a double take. He's still naked. What's more, he's not alone.

There's another figure in the Beamer, this one female. Also naked. She's crouched on the floor of the car, her head in the guy's lap, and Mona doesn't need a Muni map to know what's going on.

Mona rings the bell to get the gripman's attention, but she's laughing so hard she can't tell him what's happening. She points down at the car, but the gripman is too far away to see.

The light changes. The Beamer jerks a couple of times. Then it peels away from the intersection and, weaving from side to side, disappears from sight.

The Gripman's Way

Sam Spade, that quintessential San Francisco individualist, lived by a strict code of honor. But that code was his own, not necessarily society's. Or for that matter, the law's.

Like Sam Spade, San Francisco gripmen have their own code, their own standards and rules of behavior. If at times the Gripman's Way conflicts with the Official Rules, gripmen assume it's the Rules that are wrong.

They talk about the cable cars in proprietary language that leaves no doubt about their sense of ownership. The cable cars are theirs, period. No one else knows this antiquated machinery the way they do. No one else, especially (they'll tell you) the suits in their cushy offices, understands the feel of wet pavement beneath soft Douglas fir brakes. No one else, especially the suits, understands the effect of a new cable, or the feel of a splice as it runs through the grip. If the gripman decides his car is ready for a grip change, or the brakes need adjusting, then that's the way it's going to be. In their worldview, the responsibility is always theirs.

Rory consistently refused to take Car 11.

Each morning, when gripmen pull their empty cars out of the barn, the first thing they do is test and adjust the brakes, tightening or loosening them as needed. Most of them make this test on the block of Washington from Mason to Powell, the first block from the pull-out gate.

"It's a very slight grade," Rory explains. "So just before Powell, I'll have the conductor put his rear brake on full. If that rear brake won't hold the car, empty like that, I go right back around the block to the barn and get a different car."

He makes a face. "I kept turning in Car 11 for nearly ten years, and it was never fixed."

Their belief in responsibility is curiously old-fashioned; they have little or no patience for people who reject responsibility — for others, for themselves. That includes deadbeat fathers, welfare cheats, or for that matter the occasional lazy gripman or incompetent conductor. It also includes panhandlers and street people, alcoholics and drug addicts. They are great believers in the pull-yourself-together school of self-help. Old-fashioned virtues, old-fashioned vices.

They will remind you, too, that responsibility requires authority — and few of them are shy about asserting it.

Especially when it comes to passenger management. Because, in addition to manhandling antique machinery, one of a gripman's primary jobs is crowd control. On a jammed cable car — and most of them are — getting passengers arranged is a lot more complicated than it sounds.

People want to stand in doorways — which blocks other passengers from getting on and off. They want to stand in the "yellow zone" behind the gripman — which puts them directly in his way when he pulls back on the brake. They want to drape their arms over the back of the bench — which puts their elbows on a collision course with the track-brake handle. They want to stand up in front of the passenger bench instead of down on the running board — which blocks the gripman's view of traffic. And they don't, they absolutely don't, want to be herded into the compartment.

Each gripman has his own method of asserting control. Jamal starts out stern from the get-go. "It works better that way," he insists. Like most gripmen, Jamal is ex-military, and it shows. "The military teaches you that if you run a loose ship and you try to tighten up, you're an asshole. If you run a tight ship and then you loosen up, you're a nice guy."

Other gripmen have other means of maintaining control. Omar appreciates the uses of speed. "Sometimes speed's not such a bad thing," he says. "If you've got people on the car who want to get a little loose, letting it out a little going downhill kind of keeps them in their place, lets 'em realize who the boss is."

Passengers don't always accept the gripman's authority easily. Some of them argue; some of them glare and grumble; others are masters of passive resistance.

"A lot of European tourists will just stare at you when you tell them to move in-

The bright square directly behind the gripman is the "yellow zone."

side," Terrell says. "They try to pretend they don't understand what you're saying." It doesn't work. "You just keep pointing inside, and eventually they give up."

> The man in the yellow zone had a stubborn smile pasted on his face.
> "You have to move inside," Jake informed him.
> "Ja." The man beamed and nodded and didn't move a muscle.
> "Inside." Jake made shooing motions with his hands.
> "Ja." The man beamed and smiled and still didn't move.
> Jake isn't famous for his patience. He advanced on the man until he was chest to chest, herding him backward by sheer proximity. Finally, when the man's toes had cleared the doorway, Jake slammed the door shut on him, none too gently.
> Unfortunately, he didn't notice that the man was still gripping the edge of the doorway until he'd nipped his fingers between jamb and rubber door bumper.
> "Hey, you jerk, you smashed my fingers in the door!" the man shouted — in perfect American English.

For Drew, it was the guy in the suit.

It was an expensive suit; in fact, everything about him was expensive. And his body language let it be known that he wasn't accustomed to taking orders from the kind of guy who wore a Muni uniform.

He ignored Drew's polite "Inside the cabin please." He ignored it a second time. Finally, with a look of disgust, he eased his body into the doorway of the cabin. But the minute Drew turned back to the controls, the man took two steps forward, out of the cabin and into the yellow zone.

Drew didn't turn around. He simply took a firm hold on the grip and pulled, throwing his full 250 pounds back as far as the grip would go. There was a sharp "oof" sound behind him, and the man in the yellow zone disappeared, propelled straight back into the cabin.

Still without turning, Drew smiled gently, reached behind him and quietly pulled the cabin door shut.

Faced with a similar situation, Gervase let the cable do the job for him.

This one, too, wore an expensive suit, and carried an expensive briefcase to go with it. Three times Gervase asked him to step inside the cabin; three times the man grudgingly backed up, then stepped up into the yellow zone again the minute Gervase turned away.

Gervase though about it for a minute as the cable car idled at an intersection. When the light changed, he pulled the grip back — hard. The cable car lurched forward; the man in the suit lurched backward. He went one direction; his briefcase went another, broke open, and scattered papers across the cable car and out into the street.

"Oh, too bad," Gervase said sympathetically as the cable car glided up California Street.

Most gripmen try not to be rigid about it, and when a car is truly crowded they'll cut people some slack.

"Yeah, you can do that," Chuck agrees. "What you never do is let someone become belligerent, because if you have a person who's doing that, they're trying to take over the car. And if the car's not under our control it's dangerous. So we don't let them do that."

He permits himself a small grin. Chuck is well over six feet tall, with a background in karate. "They can be as threatening as they want," he says, "and then they have to go away."

Cable Car Confidential

Throwing People Off the Car

If they don't behave, they don't ride. Every gripman has had passengers who had to be removed from the cable car one way or another.

In the Good (or Bad) Old Days, Adam recalls nostalgically, it was a lot simpler — if a gripman wanted them off, they were off. "We used to knock 'em out, kick 'em out, shove 'em out, throw 'em off. Whatever it took."

In today's litigious world, of course, things are less simple. Gripmen are not permitted to physically lay hands on a passenger; if there's trouble, regulations tell them to call central control, and/or the police. But however they get it done, the principle still applies — if the gripman decides you need to go, you go.

The man who climbed aboard the cable car at Powell and Sutter was ready to party, carrying a drink in one hand and a lit cigar in the other.

> To cars that dive in front of a moving cable car: "If you knew what I had for brakes, you wouldn't cut in front of me."

"Sorry, you can't get on with that," the conductor informed him. "No open drinks, and no smoking on the cable car."

"Yeah, okay." The man was clearly annoyed, but he downed the drink and tossed the plastic cup toward the curb. He looked at the cigar, looked at the conductor, looked back at the cigar.

Then he put the lit cigar carefully in his pocket, giving new meaning to the term "smoking jacket." It took a call to the police to get him off the car, still smoldering gently as they took him away.

Most of the time that's the way they play it — by the book. But sometimes a more creative solution presents itself.

Linc was running the Cal line one night with four good ol' boys from Tennessee, in San Francisco for, believe it or not, a farm convention. They were outbound toward Van Ness, a nice cheerful trip — until the middle-aged man staggered aboard.

He was neoclassic drunk — wasted, slobbering, noisy, and abusive. He made sloppy passes at two women sitting on the bench; he made racist remarks to Linc; he yelled incomprehensible insults at the guys from Tennessee. And Linc's attempts to quiet him down only made him more cantankerous.

"Why don't you just kick him off?" one of the Tennesseans asked finally.

Linc sighed. "Because I'm not allowed to physically do that."

The guy from Tennessee nodded his understanding. "What happens if we do it?" he asked.

"Wellll," Linc said judiciously, "I have to admit, I have pretty bad eyesight." He pulled the car to a stop at Montgomery and leaned back against the bench.

"Okay, pal." All four Tennesseans stood up and surrounded the drunk.

"Lemme alone." The drunk flailed his arms. The Tennesseans ignored his protests. They picked him up bodily, carried him off the cable car to the curb, and deposited him none too gently on the pavement.

"Now you just sit there until you sober up," one of them said, "and leave people alone."

After which, to the wild applause of the other passengers, they quietly returned to the cable car.

Which is not to say that gripmen have never gotten physical with troublemakers, if that's what it takes to assert their authority.

In 1970, the turntable at Powell and Market was open to the sidewalk, not neatly defined by rope and concrete as it is today. Passengers milled around, and even on, the turntable waiting to board, and when the cable car pulled up, the passengers were expected to help turn it around.

Back then, Angelo was a conductor. He was also a young ex-Marine with an attitude and maybe, he admits, a bit of a short fuse.

He'd left the car to run into a nearby shop for a cup of coffee. When he came out, he found a group of sailors on and around the car, having a little fun. They were drunk, they had shore leave in San Francisco, and they'd decided the cable car made a fine merry-go-round.

Angelo yelled at them to stop. They ignored him. He yelled at them again. Then they made the mistake of laughing at him.

Angelo doesn't exactly remember how it played out, but he remembers how it ended.

"When the gripman finally grabbed me," he recalls, "there was one sailor on the ground, two sailors hanging from my left hand, and one hanging from my right."

🚋 🚋 🚋

Lloyd was on the Hyde line in the middle of the afternoon, just starting up the hill from Northpoint. In front of him, two guys in an old Ford Falcon had reached just the right level of drunken imbecility. While one guy drove, the other began throwing beer bottles out the car window at the cable car.

Well, what's a gripman to do? Lloyd grins.

"We just hooked onto the back of their car and pushed them all the way up the hill," he explains lightly.

The drunks in the car weren't amused; suddenly it wasn't so much fun anymore. They shouted profanities and shook their fists out the car windows. Lloyd just set the grip, leaned back, and laughed at them as they proceeded slowly up the hill at nine and a half miles an hour.

Along the length of the Hyde Street hill, pedestrians stopped to watch the unusual sight, but none of them took

The long, long hill -- Hyde Street from Bay to Chestnut.

it seriously. "I guess they figured we were making a movie," Lloyd suggests.

By the time the odd coupling reached Chestnut, the two drunks were furious. And it was here that they put themselves in contention for the unclear-on-the-concept award. Determined not to let themselves be pushed around by this silly-looking vehicle, they steadied their little compact Falcon in front of the *six-ton* cable car, and — with hilarious faith in Detroit technology — threw on the emergency brake.

"We pushed them all the way up to Lombard," Lloyd says, laughing, "before they finally managed to pull away."

Bike-hitching is one of those fun-for-the-feeble-minded activities that cable cars seem to engender. You pedal up to a cable car, grab hold of a bar, and let it pull you uphill. Or at least, you do until the gripman spots you.

Manny's car was outbound on Powell Street, heading up the hill at Bush, when the kid on the bike caught up with them. He grabbed hold of the bar at the edge of the doorway with his right hand, keeping a wobbly grip on his handlebars with his left.

"Hey, man, let go," Manny yelled at him. He slowed the car as much as he dared.

Pause for a short lesson in cable car dynamics. If a cable car is forced to stop halfway up a hill, the gripman is supposed to back it down to the bottom and start over. That's because starting a cable car from a dead stop, mid-hill, is both a dangerous and a supremely difficult maneuver.

About another gripman who refused to take out a car he'd previously had an accident in: "Well, I guess there are gripmen, and then there are grip_boys_."

The difficulty factor is being able to ease the brake off, and the grip on, working the car up to speed in slow, agonizingly careful increments. The danger isn't that the cable might slip out — just the opposite. The danger is that, with the entire weight of the car dropped onto the cable all at once, the soft metal of the grip and the hard metal of the cable can fuse together into a weld, causing what's called a "jump," in which the cable car goes instantly from zero to nine and a half miles an hour. It may not sound like much, but a full-out jump can send passengers flying off the car like skeet.

It can be done, of course, and some gripmen do it, under the right circumstances. These include extensive experience, dry, temperate weather, a well-seasoned cable, a sweet grip, and excellent muscle control.

On this particular evening, for whatever reason, Manny didn't like his chances. He didn't want to stop, and he didn't want to back it down. But he also didn't want to let the bicyclist get the better of him.

He yelled at the kid again. "Let go!"

"Fuck you," the kid replied.

Manny took one step toward the doorway. He raised his booted foot. The kid sneered at him. Manny kicked out, hard, at the hand on the pole.

A second later, all that could be heard was a high-pitched "Uhhnn!" from the kid as he disappeared from view, and the sound of bicycle parts clattering downhill.

🚃 🚃 🚃

Arnold was outbound on the Cal line with a crowded car, heading up the steep hill from Grant to Stockton. He was just nearing the crest when the car stuck; suddenly, Arnold found himslf wrestling with a cable car determined to roll backward.

Near the crests of the steeper hills, there are safety latches under the pavement designed to prevent a full backward runaway. But if you slide back against one of them, your cable car will have to be towed up over the crest. Besides, Arnold points out, "if you hit that safety latch too hard people go exploding out into the street."

Safety latches at California and Stockton.

He tried to set the brake, but it refused to hold; and as the car continued to slip, the only thing Arnold could do was offload his passengers to lighten the load.

"We're having a problem," he called to the passengers. "There's no need to panic, but I need you all to step off the car and go to the sidewalk."

Sensibly, everyone did as asked. Everyone, that is, except the angry-looking woman in the power suit. She was, Arnold says, "dressed for intimidation, with the collar and the briefcase and the whole nine yards. And she was really cranky."

"I'm not getting off this car," she snapped.

"Ma'am, you have to get off," Arnold repeated.

"If I get hurt out in that street," she said, glaring at him, "you're going to be up shit creek."

Arnold felt the cable car lurch backward. He felt the brake begin to slip. He hauled back on the brake handle as he spoke.

"Lady," he said, "I am already up shit creek." His muscles strained. "Step off right now or I'll have my conductor take you off and put you on the sidewalk."

Rows of cable cars tucked up in the barn.

She stood up, still angry. "I better get my same seat back when we get back on," she snapped as she finally stepped off the car.

With the car empty at last, Arnold managed to wrestle it over the crest onto flat ground, and the passengers climbed back aboard, the angry woman among them. But instead of returning to her original seat, she perched on the front bench, glaring steadily at Arnold.

Arnold knew he should let it go. He really should. But as the conductor came forward to collect fares, he couldn't help himself.

"Hey, Eddie," he said, "did that ugly woman get her seat back?"

The woman twisted around to confront him. "I heard that!"

"Oh, excuse me, ma'am," Arnold said politely. "I wasn't talking about you. There's another ugly woman sitting in the back."

The Sam Spades of the world handle their own problems, take care of their own business. And the gripman's business doesn't end at the running board. It extends to every aspect of the cable cars, from turntables to tickets. It also includes looking out for each other.

Jake, of course, wouldn't have it any other way.

California Street between Drumm and Davis is a narrow stretch of street lined with high-rise office towers. When delivery trucks double park, which most of them do, it can be very close quarters for a cable car, especially if the driver neglects to tuck in his side-view mirror.

This particular truck hadn't, but Derek thought he could just about make it. He realized he was wrong when the front edge of the cable car banged into the protruding mirror and snapped it off.

When the truck driver finally showed up, he and Derek jawed at each other for a bit, and finally Derek decided it wasn't worth it. They could file reports, and attend hearings, and argue with insurance companies, or they could settle it between them. Derek shrugged, gave the truck driver two hundred dollars to cover the damage, and forgot about the whole incident.

Until a few weeks later, when he was called in for a disciplinary hearing. The truck driver, it seems, had filed a complaint with Muni that a cable car had broken his mirror and driven away without stopping.

Enter Jake, who never met a windmill he wouldn't tilt at.

Jake didn't think what happened to his co-worker was quite fair. And then one day he saw the same truck parked on California at Montgomery, with its back door rolled up and the driver nowhere in sight.

"I noticed that the guy had left the back of his truck unlocked, and I was worried for him," Jake says, deadpan. He thought about this for a minute. Then he turned the grip over to his conductor and trotted a block down to Walgreen's.

"I bought myself a nice little five-dollar lock,"Jake explains, "and I came back, and I locked up the guy's truck for him."

Then, still deadpan: "I was looking around to see where he was, and unfortunately the key slipped out of my hand and went down into the sewer. I was a little bit embarrassed about my clumsiness, so I just walked on down to the end." He grins. "That's four blocks away, and when the guy got back to his truck you could hear him screaming from all the way down there."

In the end, a letter was written to the truck driver's company accusing him of the fraud, signed by seven cable car operators, and he was fired soon afterwards.

The gripman's responsibility, as far as they're concerned, also includes scalpers, pickpockets, and any other forms of human lice that might infest their domain.

To the driver of a car that swerved onto the tracks: "Hey, you! Out of the gene pool!"

Actually, the word "scalpers" is inaccurate. The scruffy types hanging around the turntables selling "cable car tickets" to unsuspecting tourists aren't scalpers — they're scam artists. That's because those "tickets" they're selling are in fact nothing but throwaway receipts.

Like everything else about the cable cars, fares are handled the old-fashioned way — you simply pay your two dollars, in cash, to the conductor on the car. In exchange, the conductor hands you a blue piece of paper. This is a receipt, not a ticket. Some people keep them as souvenirs; most throw them away. It's most often these discarded scraps of paper that scalpers sell as "tickets."

That's what the scalper at Powell and Market was doing, and he didn't want anyone else working his marks. There was a kid there working the line of tourists selling incense, and the scalper was giving him a hard time.

Like all gripmen, Justin hated scalpers. Scalpers offend their sense of justice, and trespass on their turf. So when he spotted the guy, he warned him off. The scalper wasn't impressed; words were exchanged; and, finally, Justin punctuated his point with a brisk right to the scalper's jaw. So brisk, in fact, that the scalper's teeth popped out and went flying across the turntable. The scalper, demoralized, fled the scene, and Justin forgot about the incident.

Until a couple of months later. Justin was back at Powell and Market, sitting peacefully on his car with a cup of coffee, when the scalper reappeared. This time, the scalper had a knife.

"He just came out of nowhere, stabbed him, and took off running," another gripman recalls. "If he'd gotten him six inches to the left he might've done some serious damage." The gripman shakes his head, not in horror but in bemusement. Weird things happen, is all. You just suck it up and move on.

Most gripmen agree that the pickpocket infestation isn't as bad as it used to be, but a number of them still carry handcuffs — if they catch 'em, they'll hold 'em. But sometimes even the most motivated gripman can't do it himself.

Barney recalls the day he had two separate teams of pickpockets on his car at the same time.

"They were working independently," he says. "They were so busy they were probably picking each other's pockets."

He stopped the car for a brief word with his conductor, who got on the radio to central control.

"You better send an army of cops down here," the conductor told them. "We're not moving until you get these pickpockets off here."

And while they waited, the pickpockets continued to do what pickpockets do, right up until the police arrived to cart them all away.

"They were too busy to notice," Barney explains, laughing. "Pickpockets are the most *distracted* people."

From one gripman to another: "I almost didn't recognize you. You look real good in men's clothes."

And then there's that particular species of human waste that gripmen refer to as "mashers."

"They're mostly old guys," Adam explains with deep disgust. "They get next to ladies and they mash up against them." He makes a face. "A lot of them like little girls."

Unfortunately, their victims rarely complain. Sometimes they're too embarrassed; sometimes they think it's accidental contact. But gripmen know it when they see it, and nothing gets someone thrown off a cable car faster.

Even if it's one of their own.

Gervase stood aside as the Japanese tour group arranged itself throughout the cable car at California and Drumm, waiting until they were settled before getting on the car.

That's when he noticed his conductor, standing on the running board, rubbing himself up and down against a young Japanese girl.

"Hey." He reached the car in two long steps and grabbed the man's arm. "What the hell are you doing?"

"Hey, don't worry about it." The conductor shrugged. "They don't mind. They like it."

"What?!" Gervase was first dumbfounded, then furious. "Man, you are one sick puppy, and you need to go. Now."

And go he did.

And sometimes... well, sometimes sick calls to sick.

The guy was a regular. Half the gripmen on the line had thrown him off their cars at one time or another. "In fact," Whit recalls, "he'd been beaten up by a couple of husbands for mashing up against their wives."

So Whit wasn't surprised when he spotted him up to his old tricks, on the running board, rubbing himself against a frowsy woman in a tight dress.

"Hey, buddy, I told you about that." Whit stopped the cable car and confronted him. "Get the hell off my car."

The masher shrugged and started to step down.

Until the woman glared at Whit and said: "Hey, c'mon. Can't a gal have some fun around here?"

And off they went, arm in arm.

The Tintinnabulation of the Bells

The sound of the cable car bells may be as famous as the chimes of Big Ben. In the hands of a talented gripman, the big, solid-brass bell on the roof of each cable car can squeeze a grin out of a stone and set solemn business-men to two-stepping along the sidewalks. They are the quintessential sound of San Francisco.

In fact, though, there are two different kinds of bells on each cable car. And neither of them is there strictly for entertainment.

The famous ones — the "bell-ringing" bells on the outside of the car — are simply the nineteenth-century equivalent of the automobile horn. They signal the cable car's arrival; they warn automobiles off the tracks; they call out drivers of double-parked trucks.

The second bell, smaller and unpre-possessing, is inside the cable car, attached to the ceiling over the gripman's head. A rope is threaded back from the front of the car through the compartment to the conductor's station at the rear. Instead of a great clanging sound, the inside bell makes a weak, totally unmusical clatter. This bell is used to communicate between gripman and conductor.

That's why, if you want to get off the cable car at the next stop, you tell the operator. You do not, ever, pull that handy bell rope overhead, even though it looks exactly like the signal cord on a bus.

If you hear a conductor say "two bells," (or sometimes "ding ding") he's telling the gripman the car is ready to move out. And if you hear three quick bells, hang on to your pole.

The bell code:

One bell: Stop for passengers getting off.
Two bells: Ready to proceed.
Three bells: Stop immediately.
Four bells: Clear to back down the hill.

The Learning Curve

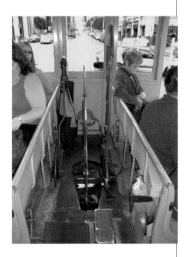

Any Muni driver is eligible to sign up for cable car training. But of the dozens who try it each year, less than thirty percent eventually stand in the slot as full-fledged gripmen. Some of them aren't strong enough; some aren't mentally quick enough; some are simply not fearless enough.

The ones who do make it are special. More to the point, they know they're special.

They're perversely proud of the difficulty factor.

"You've got to be some kind of an athlete," Barry says. "When I came to work here, I could pull 360 pounds. That's just not something your average person can do."

In fact, the job of cable car gripman is strikingly similar to that of a high-level professional athlete.

It is a tremendously difficult job that only a minuscule portion of the population can do, a job compounded of physical and mental skills.

Like professional sports, gripping requires the highest level of physical dexterity, the ability to concentrate on six things at once, the willingness to play hurt. There's hardly a gripman alive who hasn't had multiple work-related injuries, multiple surgeries, multiple physical problems.

The physical demands are one reason some gripmen choose one cable car line over another.

The California line cars are bigger, heavier, and "a son-of-a-bitch to stop," Whit says. "You work five hours with them, you feel like you've worked fifteen. You just have to muscle them too much."

On the other hand, some operators, especially conductors, move to the Cal line to escape the turntables, which — like everything else about the cable cars — are operated by sheer human muscle power. And shoving a loaded turntable a dozen times a day plays hell with the human back and the human knee.

"I about couldn't walk, my back was so bad," Derek recalls. "Then I went over to the Cal line a year ago, and I feel like a new man."

Still, while gripmen are subject to a wide range of injuries, operating a cable car actually seems to be less hazardous to one's overall wellbeing.

Every Muni operator, bus or streetcar or cable car, has to pass the same medical clearance. "And usually," Barry reports, "the cable car guys come through a lot healthier than the bus drivers. Very seldom do you see ones with a lot of high blood pressure. We don't keep our butts in the seat all day long. We get to move around."

Back in 1999, the California line was shut down for repairs for three months. And at the start, the buses that replaced it were driven by cable car operators.

By the time the shutdown ended, nearly all the bus drivers were — bus drivers.

Every cable car operator who could manage it was gone. They took vacation time; they took comp time; they scheduled elective surgeries. They did anything they could think of to get them off the buses. And every one of the ones who remained reported feeling worse, and having more physical problems, than they had while operating the cable cars.

Besides excellent physical condition, it also helps if you're a bit of an extrovert. Because gripmen, like athletes, perform on a public stage, standing high in the slot in their open-air vehicles. Wide-eyed tourists watch their every move; pedestrians turn and follow their progress with admiring smiles as the cable car glides by. Nobody doesn't notice a cable car.

Gripmen understand this.

"A cable car's like an amusement, an entertainment," Rico says, "like going to Disneyland."

"We know we're being watched," Benjy admits, "but we have to rise above that."

"If you can't be on television or in movies," Marshall says, grinning, "this is the best place to be."

Cable car training begins with a fast walkthrough in the barn, where prospective gripmen spend not much more than three or four hours being shown the mysteries of cable car mechanics. Next is the training car, where they stand in the slot of a real cable car, on a real street, for the first time. Even with no passengers and a supportive trainer, the experience can be unnerving.

Adam, like most experienced gripmen, is cheerfully unsympathetic. "When they get behind these controls," he says, "all of a sudden it hits them like a load of bricks — this is for real. If I mess up it's going to hurt me."

He points to the controls. "If you pull the track brake handle wrong, the latch comes down and traps your skin, and you get a great big blood blister on your hand. If you step on the foot brake wrong, it can take all the skin off your leg from the ankle all the way up to the knee." He grins. "You can also fall through the grip hole, and you can imagine how uncomfortable that can be."

This is the point at which a certain number of trainees walk away — sometimes abruptly.

"I've seen people leave these in the middle of the street and walk away from them, with blood dripping off of both hands and tears coming out of both eyes, never looking back." Adam laughs. "I mean, that was it, the whole job, they just went, whoa."

And finally, there is line training — taking the controls of a cable car carrying real passengers, under the jaundiced eye of an experienced gripman.

Gripmen aren't required to accept trainees, and many of them refuse, often because of bad experiences in the past. Many former line trainers complain that trainees they flunked were accepted anyway.

The ones who agree to be line trainers are guys who'd feel right at home calling cadence in a Roman galley.

"It doesn't take much for me to wash them out," Luke says. "If I don't like their attitude I'll wash them out. Like if they're hot-dogging out there. If I find two or three different things that he does — if he's skinning rope, or if he can't handle a back-down — he's gone."

He shakes his head. "I'll spend a lot of time on some guy, and when he's on his own a month later I see him flying down the hill, or pulling into the barn and sitting in the yard for two hours, brand-new guys."

"It takes an old-fashioned hardhead to operate these things," Whit agrees, "but what you've got to do in the training process is smooth that hardness out a little bit."

If you want to judge how well a gripman is operating, watch how much work he *doesn't* do.

Notice especially on a steep downhill run, and you'll see that the best gripmen aren't constantly hauling on their levers, messing with the grip or tightening and releasing the brake. The best of them will simply engage the grip completely and then relax, letting the machinery do the work. "That's the most work-efficient way to operate these cars," Lloyd explains.

"Some of us operate at about fifty percent of our capability," he says. "We have a lot of reserve. Whereas some of these guys operate at closer to ninety percent, so they don't have any reserve if things get rough."

Conductors go through the same kind of training. In fact, a gripman is not automatically qualified to be a conductor unless he's been trained for it. And conductors too need to be in good physical condition.

Adam recalls one conductor-trainee who was "so fat he just sort of rolled."

One of a conductor's tasks is pulling switches, which are set into slots in the pavement. This guy couldn't even do that.

"He would actually be flat on the ground, all the way on the ground, to pull it," Adam laughs. "He lasted about half a day."

Working the cable cars can also require personal sacrifice that not all applicants are willing to endure.

Cable car barn
and museum
at Mason
and Washington

She'd been driving buses, but thought she'd give cable car conducting a try. She walked into the barn on her first day, climbed onto the back of a Powell line car, and checked out the equipment. She looked at the brake mechanism. She looked at her inch-long, bright-red fingernails. She looked back at the brake one more time.

Then she shook her head, climbed off the car, and returned to the buses.

Why do they choose the cable cars? There are as many reasons as there are gripmen, but one theme that repeats over and over is freedom — freedom from the rigid, confining, soul-deadening routine of the buses. Not just physical freedom, but personal freedom. There's something about the cable car division ...

Barry calls it "the foreign legion outpost of the Muni railway," the Last Chance Hotel for drivers on the edge. Cable cars are where, if you had to go there, they had to take you in. If, that is, you could do the job.

"Somebody had a problem somewhere else, they sent 'em to cable cars," he says.

They particularly exiled drivers who, to put it politely, "had trouble with authority."

"Back in the sixties," Linc recalls, "they used to send guys over here who got into trouble with their supervisors, guys who were basically anti-authority."

"They would send people over here that had a problem keeping their license, they might have had a medical problem, or they just didn't like authority," Angelo says. "Then when they got to the cable cars they found a home. They worked hard; they came here and they did work. The only problem was, when they tried to pass some bullcrap on them, they wouldn't go for it."

"And the thing is," Theo points out, "that sets a tone, you know? New guys come over, and they get socialized into the same sort of attitudes.

"What happens is, you get a self-regulating system; that's how people are socialized into it. So even operators who weren't necessarily troublemakers develop this really independent streak."

The term for those who don't is "houseboy," perhaps the single worst insult one can apply to a cable car operator.

It's a tough crowd to try to intimidate. Barry offers some numbers, and a theory. "In 1976, seven of every ten operators out here were — guess what? You got it, Marines. We have some Korean vets, and some Vietnam vets. And the others were paratroopers, or special forces, or professional athletes. Now that says something about the job."

Many of them have disciplinary jackets an inch thick, and don't care. At least half the operators interviewed for this book were willing to have their real names used, and damn the consequences.

"I was ready to quit Muni," one young gripman said. "I hated getting up in the morning, hated going to work in the morning." He decided to give cable cars a try before quitting. "Now," he says, "I love going to work every day."

Another rookie admitted that "if I'd stayed on the buses, I'd have wound up punching someone."

Of course, some drivers chose cable cars simply because gripmen had more fun.

"A friend of mine was here," Angelo recalls, "and he said, you gotta come over here, man, the women are crazy. It's party all the time." He laughs. "This was back in the early seventies, when there were groupies, and parties, and you could pick up an Irish coffee at one end of the run and drink it on the way down."

Jackson definitely didn't want to be a gripman.

"I used to do nothing but the bus," he says. "When I thought about the cable cars, I thought, oh no, I don't want to do that."

Then, in the early eighties, he decided he wanted to be an inspector.

"I wanted to work in all the barns, so I'd know the equipment. So I went over to the cable car barn, so that if they sent me over there as an inspector I'd have some idea of what I was doing."

He pauses, searching for the right words, and after a minute or two he shrugs and looks sheepish.

"I came over here," he says finally, "and fell in love."

Several operators also mention the people factor.

Muni bus drivers sit in a three-walled cubicle, under a sign that reads: "Information gladly given, but safety prohibits unnecessary conversation." To the average gregarious gripman, this qualifies as cruel and unusual punishment.

"I like the fact that you're a lot closer to people," Eugene says. "And you also have a conductor, so there are two of us, and that's real nice."

"I think the people are the real difference," Cam says thoughtfully. "The ones who ride the cable cars are on vacation. They're here because they want to have a good time."

Kent even appreciates the locals. "We've got the best public in the world," he says. "San Francisco people are cool — they're very peaceful, very relaxing to be around." He grins. "I used to prefer tourists, but you get a little older and wiser and more mature."

Rookie Mistakes

No matter how much training a gripman gets before he's sent out on the line, there are things he can only learn through experience. Sometimes hard experience.

Barney and Grover were both rookies, working together on the Cal line. The cable car was stopped for the red light at Kearny, and now Barney waited, his hand resting lightly on his grip. In front of him, a cab idled at the intersection.

"That rope was hot, really hot," Barney recalls. "I smelled this odor, sort of bad. And I heard the grip growling, but I didn't know what it meant."

The light changed. Barney moved the grip.

"The cable car jumped maybe four feet off the ground, and I tore the back right off that cab."

Shaken, Barney slammed on the brakes and looked around. "Everyone okay?" he called out. The passengers, most of them locals, agreed they were fine. The cab driver, shaken but unhurt, emerged from his cab to inspect the damage. Barney breathed a sigh of relief.

Until a woman came forward from the back of the cable car and called to him. "You'd better come back here," she told him.

At the back end of the car, Grover was crumpled in the grip hole, not moving.

Barney raced across the street to the Bank of America building and called central control, which promised to send out an ambulance — and of course an inspector. Barney raced back across the street to the cable car.

There was Grover, sitting up and checking himself to see if all his moving parts were still moving.

"And that," Barney explains, "was my first jump."

There's an emergency maneuver referred to as "walking a car downhill," in which the car is moved by alternately applying and releasing the brakes. Sane gripmen only do this in two circumstances — when they've lost the cable, or when they need to go downhill more slowly than cable speed. In any other situation, coming down a steep hill is done at full grip. "Because," as Justin put it, "it's better to hit something at nine and a half miles an hour than to hit it at forty-five miles an hour."

Add to the inherent risks the added elements of rain, inexperience, and the Hyde Street hill, and what you have could be lethal.

> Q: what's the new guy's name?
>
> A: Rookie.
>
> Q: But what's his name?
>
> A: That's his name. When I call out, "Rookie," he answers.

Purley's cable car had just reached Chestnut when the cable dropped out of the grip. He stopped there and looked down the hill; only three blocks to the end of the line.

With no cable, Purley determined to walk the car down on its brakes.

Now this is not only violently against cable car regs, it's a maneuver that even the most experienced gripmen would reject as total insanity. And, as Purley proved, they'd be right.

The car — loaded with passengers — headed downhill, picking up speed as it went. The brakes slipped on the wet track.

And halfway down the hill, unable to control the car, Purley jumped off the car, leaving the passengers on an unattended roller coaster which plowed into a station wagon at Bay Street.

Yes, of course he got fired.

Houseboy* in the House

—By a Gripman

I cannot take a headway now, cause I am not like you,
  I love to snitch, I'll be your bitch, I'm houseboy through and
  through.
I have to run, I cannot wait or I'll get written up,
  The TLC is watching me, I've got to kiss some butt.
Oh dispatcher hey, please make my day and put me on Run Nine,
  While on my split I'll take your shit and give your shoes a
  shine.
Just call me up at any time and I'll come in to work,
  I have no life but Muni stuff; I'm such a bleeping jerk.
I can't pull in or call in sick because they'll think I'm bad,
  I must look good for management or else I'll make them mad.
I'm prideful of my ignorance; I've never learned the ropes,
  My fellow workers hate my ass; I'm such a bleeping dope.
I've never had a PSR because I'm cute and good,
  But I must work at cable cars; they'd kill me in the hood.
      Don't know my kids,
        Don't know my wife,
          But I'll pull in on time,
            And if you all make fun of me,
      Some time I'll drop the dime.

                    © by the gripman who wrote it

* "Houseboy" is the term Muni operators give to employees who side
  with management againt their fellow workers.

Silly Gripmen's Tricks

Sometimes, of course, even gripmen have moments of just plain silliness.

"Well, who knew she'd do it?" Terrell defends himself.

Like so many tourists, the middle-aged woman didn't realize that the line of cable cars sitting at California and Drumm were on layover on the eastbound track, rather than being the next to leave. She climbed aboard the last car in line just as the next westbound car passed by.

"When does the cable car leave?" she asked.

"This isn't the next car," Terrell said. "That one is." He pointed to the car as it passed. "If you want the next car," he joked, "you'll have to run and catch up with it."

And before he could say another word, the woman had taken off, purse flapping against her side, giving a creditable imitation of a marathon runner as she raced up California Street after the moving cable car.

Drew never met a pretty girl he didn't like. So when the red Mustang pulled alongside his cable car at Kearny and California one Sunday morning, he just naturally got into conversation with the two blondes inside. Since he had a trainee at the grip, he swung around to the running board and leaned out toward them.

"Hey, you folks should let the top down on a beautiful day like this," he called out.

"We don't know how." The driver cocked her head and made helpless motions with her hands.

"It's easy." Drew jumped off the cable car, leaned into the Mustang and pushed the button. Then he climbed back aboard and grinned down at them.

"Thanks!" The blondes were enthusiastically grateful. When the light changed, they paced the cable car for another block, giggling and flirting.

"You know what?" Drew said when they stopped for the light at Montgomery. "I'd look real good in that car with you guys."

"Well, hop in," the driver challenged him as the light changed.

"You don't think I would, do you?" Drew checked the street; from here to the end, it was flat and the traffic was minimal. "Okay, man, you're ready," he said to the trainee. "You take it on down to the terminal."

"You're kidding." The trainee stared at him. "You're not really going to hop in there?"

And Drew, grinning, jumped from the moving cable car into the back seat of the Mustang and rode away down California Street.

And then there's Jake.

To repeat: If you want to understand cable car gripmen, you must first understand this one thing. There are simply not enough people who can do this job. How else can one explain Jake?

Jake is an ongoing saga, the stuff of pure mythology. When Jake gets in a scrape, it becomes a vendetta. When he gets in an accident, it becomes a headline. When he plays a practical joke, it enters the annals of legend.

Jake is also, let it be noted for the record, a first-rate gripman, whose escapades may put himself in danger but never his passengers. Regular cable car riders adore him. Whenever he serves one of his many suspensions (or sits out during one of his many surgeries), people inquire anxiously about him. He seems, somehow, like a link to San Francisco past; so long as we still have people like Jake, individualism survives in Baghdad by the Bay.

He is, in a word, unique.

Powell Street between Sutter and California is narrow, precipitously steep, and heavily trafficked. To keep auto and cable car traffic separate, the cable car tracks are on a slightly raised cobblestone roadbed, complete with signs that read: Keep Off Tracks.

Powell Street approaching California — barely enough room even when it's done right.

Jake had just passed Pine Street headed uphill to California. The shiny, brand-new Cadillac on his right — so new it didn't even have license plates — had a full lane to itself but couldn't seem to stay in it. Instead, it drifted toward the cable car, so close that its tires bumped along the raised track bed. The cable car was full, which meant a full running board along the right side, and the unlucky passengers were squealing with apprehension and jumping onto the upper step as the Cadillac nearly grazed the edge of the cable car.

Jake set the grip and darted around the passengers to the right front edge of the cable car. He took a firm grip on the white-painted stanchion. Then he did what even he describes as maybe the nuttiest thing he's ever done.

As both vehicles continued on uphill, he jumped onto the hood of the Cadillac, kept his grip on the stanchion, and proceeded to execute a fairly creditable flamenco dance that stove in the Cadillac's hood in six or seven different places just as the cable car reached California Street.

This is where the Powell and California cables cross each other underground. And because the Powell cable runs below the Cal cable, Powell cars have to raise their grip up and out of the way. If they don't, the grip will collide — hard — with a bumper bar placed under the pavement to prevent a collision with the California cable.

As Jake's cable car crested at California, he performed one more quick step, jumped back on the cable car, made his let-go, and rolled to a stop without incident.

"If that driver had stopped, or even accelerated, I'd have hit that bumper bar and nothing I could've done about it." Jake shakes his head, amazed at his own craziness. "I'd have been doo-doo."(Yes, he really said "doo-doo.")

The driver of the Cadillac, totally unnerved by the apparition dancing on his hood, made a fast right at California and disappeared. But the next day, furious at the damage to his brand-new car, he showed up at the barn.

Fortunately for Jake, all the Cadillac driver had seen were stamping feet; he confronted a group of gripmen and demanded to know the name of the crazy gripman who'd destroyed his car hood.

The gripmen looked at the angry man. They looked at each other. They shook their heads.

"On the hood of the car? You mean, while the cable car's moving? At California and Powell?" They shook their heads more firmly. "You've gotta be kidding," they said at last, and a couple of glances flicked toward Jake. "Come on, nobody's that goofy."

Jake also has a particular fondness for things that go boom.

A track torpedo is a small explosive device used by railroads for signaling purposes. It is placed on the track so that when a long train backs over it, the small but noisy explosion tells the engineer when to apply his brakes. They are not, of course, used by cable cars.

Well, not usually.

Jake was waiting at the pull-out gate with the track torpedo as Jamal's cable car headed down the Washington Street hill.

"What I did was, I ran out to the track like a comedy character" — he pantomimes an exaggerated Keystone Kops move, knees high, elbows flailing — "and I wave to Jamal and bend down and put the torpedo on the track. And then I ran back to the barn the same way."

He cocks his head, looking slightly aggrieved. "Of course you'd know something's up. Except Jamal's busy talking to some pretty girl, and he doesn't see me do any of this."

Jamal, in fact, was facing the other way, with his back to the window, when Jake placed the torpedo. He was still facing backward when the car hit the torpedo with a boom! big enough to satisfy even Jake.

Jamal jumped a foot, the car hurtled the rest of the way down the hill and rammed into the bumper bar, shutting down the entire Hyde line for more than an hour.

An M-1000 is an explosive device somewhere between a large fire-cracker and a small grenade, approximately equivalent to a quarter stick of dynamite. Why Jake is carrying them, that day on the Cal line, is still open to conjecture.

The line is stopped because of a traffic jam on Nob Hill, and Jake's car is sitting at Hyde Street. Diego's car is a block back, at Larkin.

Jake is bored.

Directly in front of his car is a manhole cover. Jake ties the M-1000 to one end of a piece of string, and ties a stick to the other end. He lights a cigarette and ties it to the M-1000. He drops the M-1000 through a hole in the manhole cover so that it hangs from the string, held in place by the stick.

Then he pulls his cable car forward to the next corner and motions to Diego to move up a block behind him.

Diego pulls up to Hyde, positioning his car directly over the manhole. He sits down on the passenger bench and takes out his lunch. He takes a bite...

Boom!

Diego's sandwich flies out into the street. Diego leaps to his feet, grabs his cell phone, and frantically calls central. Get PG & E down here! We've had a major explosion! We've got a gas leak!

And Jake quietly pulls his car in to the barn.

Even if the thing that goes boom doesn't work, Jake can still find a use for it.

Jake was working the Hyde line, on a run that pulled out of the barn at 7:01 a.m. Every morning, he'd head out with a large mug of coffee, so by the time he got to Aquatic Park, nature would be calling.

And every morning, just as he pulled in, Rico would make a beeline for the operators' bathroom and take root there, leaving Jake squirming outside.

Jake finally decided to Take Steps.

The following morning, he arrived carrying an M-1000. This one was a dud — but of course Rico didn't know that.

Jake also had a length of cannon fuse — don't ask — which he at-tached to one end of the M-1000.

As usual, when Jake's cable car reached Aquatic Park, Rico went haring into the bathroom.

This time, instead of banging on the door, Jake climbed up to the roof of the bathroom. And as the other operators watched, goggle-eyed, he lit the fuse and dropped it through the vent into the bathroom.

"Dammit, Jake, what the hell are you doing?" Rico's panicky voice emerged from the bathroom, followed almost immediately by Rico himself, hauling up his pants.

Amid the general laughter, Jake asked innocently: "Well, how'd everything come out?"

Rico, sheepishly: "Faster than usual."

There are, of course, two entirely different types of cable car currently in use. The cars that run on the Hyde and Mason lines are smaller and single-ended — that is, they have a single grip mechanism, and can only (in theory) be operated in one direction. That's why they need to be turned around, on turntables, at the end of the line.

The bigger, heavier California line cars are double-ended, with full grip and brake mechanisms at each end. When a Cal car reaches the end of the line, the gripman simply walks to the other end of the car and picks up the second grip.

These two types of cars — also in theory — can *not* run on each other's lines.

Cable cars move from one line to another via a series of switches set into the pavement. To make this move, the conductor must get off the car and haul the switch handle into position. One of these switches is on Powell Street between Washington and Jackson.

Amelia was on a Cal line car, starting her last day as a conductor. She had a trainee along, and when they reached the switch, she and the trainee stepped off the car for a quick demonstration of the switch.

"You use this switch to transfer over to the Mason line," she said, pulling the handle upward to demonstrate. Unfortunately, the gripman didn't notice this hands-on lesson. Just as Amelia pulled the switch, he disengaged the track brake.

When Amelia looked up, she was treated to the sight of the big Cal car pointed inexorably toward the Bay-Taylor turntable.

California cars do not fit on the turntables. Amelia sighed and called the barn, which sent out a truck to push the car back onto its correct track. The truck came out; the driver snickered and pushed the cable car back across the switch.

They were so busy snickering, in fact, that they forgot one thing — you have to lift the switch to back across it.

The cable car broke the switch, shutting down the entire line for nearly four hours.

Cable Car Confidential

A conductor pulls the swith for a Bay-Taylor cable car at Powell and Jackson.

The most famous example of right-car/wrong-line, however, wasn't accidental.

Casey just wanted a memorable swan song, something unique for his last run before retirement. What he finally decided on was a Grand Tour of all three lines in a single evening.

Easy enough to pull out on the Hyde line and switch to the Mason line, of course. But how do you take a Hyde car onto the Cal line, when there's no turntable to reverse it?

Well, you back-grip it.

Every gripman has done an occasional spot of back-gripping — operating a cable car from the rear rather than the front — usually on a California line car when the front grip goes bad. And while it sounds easy, it's a lot more complicated than it appears.

Because you aren't just using the controls at the back end of the car, you're operating them in reverse.

"First of all," Casey pondered, "I'll be going forward. Then when I want to come back the other way, I have to be sort of at the back end of the car from the way it's moving. So I have to pull the grip this way to go that way and I have to rethink where to make the let-go's."

Casey worked it out carefully. He chose eleven o'clock at night, to minimize traffic. And he chose to reverse-grip in the westbound direction to avoid the steep downhill from Grant to Stockton.

"I didn't want to be coming down that hill trying to figure out how to stop the car so I don't run into some taxi," he says. "I didn't want to come out here and blunder, even if it was my last day and it would be difficult for them to severely punish me."

He also arranged a conductor swap to get the accomplice he wanted.

88

Casey's own photograph of his Hyde Street car at California and Van Ness.

"Your conductor has to be your eyes," he explains. "Without a good conductor you can't do it."

Once he had the process worked out to his satisfaction, he notified a few people — "real railroad buff types" — and told them: "If you're interested, you might want to pay attention to the California line on Sunday night, November eighth."

And off he went, for what turned out to be a memorable — and memorably unremarkable — run. Even the Cal line passengers didn't realize what was going on.

"Oh, yes, I was carrying passengers." Casey grins. "I was always in service."

One woman noticed, but wasn't sure what she noticed. "Is there something different about this?" she asked.

"Kind of," Casey replied. "This isn't the usual car that would be on this line."

"Oh." The woman shrugged and sat down.

If the passengers were blasé, the railroad buffs weren't. "It took almost twice as long as I thought it would," Casey recalls, "bcause various co-workers and rail fans kept insisting I stop so they could take pictures."

And the fallout? There was no fallout.

"I got a call from somebody at central," Casey reports, "but he sounded more puzzled than anything else. It didn't seem like it particularly registered on him."

His favorite coment came from a cable machinery worker: "You did a pretty good job" the man told him, "because I didn't hear about it until three days later."

About Speed

On flat ground, or going uphill, cable cars are limited by the speed of the cable to nine and a half miles an hour. Downhill, however ...

Certain gripmen are famous — or infamous — for the speed of their descents. A few are such cowboys — the gripmen's term — that some conductors refuse to work with them.

The official land-speed record for a cable car is 56 miles per hour. It's considered official because that's what the cop clocked Morty at just before he stopped him at California and Montgomery.

This was back in the Good Old Days, when the weekend traffic signals were all flashing yellows on California and flashing reds on the side streets. Coming down the hill from Stockton, Morty would time the light at Grant and, at the right moment, pop the grip and just open it up. By the time he got to Montgomery, he was flying low.

The cop wasn't amused. But when he pulled out his ticket book, Morty shook his head. The traffic code, he pointed out politely, only applied to "motorized vehicles."

Rookies are often drunk on speed. But sometimes they get over it.

"I was a cowboy when I first started — for the first two weeks," Benny recalls. "Then a lady had a heart attack on my car." He shakes his head. "I don't know if it was my fault or not — probably not, I guess — but it still made me slow down."

The long, downhill straightaways can produce the most speed, but not necessarily the biggest rush. For that, the stretch of Powell from California outbound to Jackson takes the prize, a four-block rollercoaster ride that's both fast and challenging.

So much so, that management finally announced a new set of rules. Every cable car was to make a full stop at each corner.

Some of the gripmen grumbled that they were taking all the fun out of the job. Linc, however, took it as a challenge.

"They forgot, there's no cable under there," he points out. "So you can go just as fast as gravity takes you. The fun is getting from corner to corner as fast as you can and still make a smooth stop. Blast from California to Sacramento, smooth stop. Blast from Sacramento to Clay, stop. Blast from Clay to Washington, smooth stop. That's a real challenge, harder than just opening it up from Cal to Washington without stopping." He grins. "You can get from California to Washington just as fast making your stops. But you gotta be a pro to do it."

He nods his head. "They cannot take our challenges away from us. They think they can, but they can't."

After a while, suffering fools gladly wears on even the most equable temperament. When you've been cut off in traffic three times in three blocks, or answered the same question half a dozen times, sometimes "have a good day" just doesn't cut it.

The four-block downhill run from California to Jackson Street.

Nowadays, the pointed spire of the Transamerica Pyramid is a local icon, nearly as recognizable as the Golden Gate Bridge. But when it was first built, it seemed like every tourist on the Cal line would point to it and ask what it was. Adam, bored with reality, would answer with a perfectly straight face: "Oh, that's the Egyptian consulate." (Most of them bought it, too.)

And sometimes, a gripman gets lucky and things just sort of fix themselves.

Frenchy had hit the depression beam so hard that his cable car popped off the tracks. He sighed and called Central, then settled down to wait for the inspector, the tow truck, and the inevitable ruckus.

Lon didn't know there was a derailed cable car ahead of him. He came around the downhill corner at full speed, and plowed flat-out into the back of Frenchy's car.

Lon climbed down off his car. Frenchy, whiling away the wait in a nearby bar, heard the crash and trotted outside. Two inspectors arrived. All four of them approached the derailed car.

It was sitting, blamelessly undamaged, back on its tracks.

Conductors

In his own sphere, the conductor's authority is as absolute as the gripman's, and his responsibility nearly as great. "Conductor," in fact, is an inaccurate term, because collecting fares is the least important part of the job.

The conductor's most important function is operating the rear brakes. Cable car brakes lack such twenty-first-century luxuries as hydraulics or antilock systems; they are stopped by the oldest power source in the world — human muscle. And on a good-sized hill, it takes two people to wrestle the cars to a halt.

That's why conductors, like gripmen, need space to work. And it's why conductors, like gripmen, also have to contend with crowd control.

This is especially true on the Powell Street cars, where the charm of the open-air back deck is a tourist magnet, especially to those seeing San Francisco through two-inch viewfinders. And some of them seem to think that that funny-looking brake mechanism is just there for decoration, whining and complaining if they're asked to move inside. But they complain even louder if the conductor slams into them while hauling on the brake, which is exactly what happens if the brake area isn't kept clear.

In a pinch, a gripman on a Powell line car can usually wrestle the car to a stop by himself. On the bigger, heavier California Street cars, it's pretty nearly impossible. On all three lines, keeping the rear brake area clear is a continuous hassle.

Conductors also have to help turn the turntables, get out and pull the manual switches at switchpoints, and help push the car if it misses what's called the take-rope — places where the cable (also referred to as the rope) has to be dropped and then picked up again.

There are a number of these "let-go" points on each of the lines — places where the gripman has to release the cable and let the car coast, running on gravity alone. Some of them occur where two cables cross each other; some occur where the car moves from one cable to another.

Occasionally, the cable car's downhill momentum fails before it reaches the take-rope, the spot where the grip can be re-engaged. When this happens, the cable car needs to be physically pushed forward to the correct place.

Yes, pushed. What's more, by longstanding tradition, passengers are expected to get off the car and help. This causes much amusement, especially to the gripman and conductor.

"You tell 'em to push, and they look at you wide-eyed," Grover says, laughing. "They get this look on their faces, like, yeah, right, very funny. It takes a few seconds before it dawns on them that you're serious, that they actually do have to get out and push."

"You say, men and women, we don't discriminate here, everybody pushes. I go you, you, and you look strong, come on. They stand there, like, who's gonna make the first move? It's like a school dance, nobody wants to be the first one. Because they're still not sure you're not playing some sort of practical joke on 'em."

And if you still think the conductor is nothing but a glorified ticket-taker ... well, Seth has a story for you.

The Hyde Street cable car was inbound from Aquatic Park, just starting up the steep grade from Bay to Chestnut. Middle of the afternoon, full tourist load, everyone having a good time — just another day in paradise. Only this wasn't paradise for the man sitting in his car at Chestnut, looking down the long, steep grade and contemplating suicide.

No one knows if he'd planned it out, or if it was a spur-of-the-moment decision. But as the cable car lumbered up the hill, the man pulled away from the curb, aimed the nose of his old compact at the cable car, and hit the accelerator.

The experienced gripman, seeing the car hurtling toward him, slammed on the track brake and released the cable, but there was nothing he could do to avoid the impact.

Hyde Street car comes uphill from Chestnut — what the driver saw.

They estimate the compact was doing sixty miles an hour when it crashed head-on into the front of the oncoming cable car. The gripman was hurled backward, slamming his head on the door jamb. Passengers were tossed around like pinballs. The cable car went plummeting back down the hill.

And inside the cabin, Seth, the conductor, realized that he was the only person still standing. Everyone else had fallen down — including the gripman.

"Conductors have a sense of self-preservation, of holding on at all times," he says now, deadpan.

He shoved his way to the front of the car, shouting to the gripman to get up, but when he got there he realized that wasn't going to happen. The gripman was lying on the floor bleeding, clutching his head and looking dazed.

"So I pulled the red handle." Seth shrugs, making a slot-blade stop sound easy.

(It's not. The slot-blade is the cable car's emergency brake. Pulling the red handle drives a triangular piece of metal into the cable slot underneath the car; it can ram itself into the slot so quickly that it literally fuses to the sides. It can also nearly yank an operator's arm out of its socket.)

"And a block or so later the car stopped," Seth goes on, "after hitting four or five other cars and trucks." He cocks his head. "It was a very exciting, um, about three and a half seconds.

"They made the gripman a hero," he adds, still deadpan, "and I went home."

In the end, the driver of the car was killed instantly, and thirty or more people were taken off the cable car to local hospitals. But of the people on the cable car, only the gripman himself was seriously hurt. As they put him into the ambulance, he mumbled: "Somebody has to go up and stop that man because we need to talk to him."

"I have a theory, but don't quote me because gripmen are really, really sensitive. It's about why gripmen fall down a lot in accidents. Gripmen pull on these levers all day long, so they become very topheavy. Conductors are built lower to the ground."

Of course, collecting fares is still the most visible part of the conductor's job.

Cable car fares are two dollars a ride, no transfers, no turnarounds. If you want to ride the California line from Drumm to Van Ness and back, you have to pay two dollars at Drumm, and another two dollars at Van Ness. You can also buy a variety of long-term Muni passes, including an all-day ticket for six dollars, three- and seven-day passes, and a monthly "Fast Pass" for $35 a month, which most local commuters use.

Like everything else about the cable cars, most fares are collected the old-fashioned way — in cash, by a human being. It may be the last pure cash transaction left in the modern world. And these days, the conductors take their responsibility seriously.

Which wasn't always the case. In the past, the cable car conductor's job was considered a license to steal; it was a given that conductors were thieves. And on occasion, long-time operators concede, there was some truth to it.

If you look toward the ceiling of a cable car, you'll see a system of red and white levers that don't seem to do anything. But twenty years ago, those levers were used to record fares. Each time the conductor collected a fare, he was supposed to flip a lever.

Malcolm was working the Mason line on a Saturday night, watching his conductor going through the car collecting fares. Suddenly Malcolm realized the conductor wasn't hitting the levers. "He wouldn't hit that thing once," Malcolm recalls, "because he didn't want people to be aware that he was supposed to do something." The conductor simply pocketed the money — all of it.

"That's when our daily salary was something like thirty bucks," Malcolm recalls, "and this guy bragged that he was knocking down maybe a hundred and twenty a day."

"Stealing was expected," Linc says. "Everybody in the railway thought it, and they wouldn't listen to anything else. They thought everybody out here was making grand theft money. You're on cable cars, you're a thief."

Otto started out training for the streetcars, the old PCCs that ran along Market Street. Unfortunately, he never managed to learn how to drive them — in fact, he couldn't even get the training car out of the barn. After working with him for a while, the training department threw up its collective hands and sent him to the supervisor.

"Gripmen get all the glory, plus they get all the babes. This is a tradition for 125 years now."

Otto figured he was about to be fired, but the supervisor had other ideas.

"Look," he said, "we're going to send you over to the cable cars as a conductor." Otto nodded, relieved.

"And while you're there," the supervisor added, "you see how much you can steal before they catch you."

Nowadays, cable car conductors are nearly the last city workers who are trusted to handle cash. In fact, they vie with each other to turn in the biggest pot. (The unofficial record is just under $3,000, on a Sunday afternoon on the Cal line.)

And sometimes they'll go to great lengths to get that last two-dollar fare.

The tour group at Market Street came close to filling Tim's car, but as he collected their fares from the group leader half a dozen other passengers squeezed on. When the car headed out, Tim called: "Fares, please."

Nobody responded.

> "It's fashionable among college girls to run a scam — give you ten, here's five, we're paying for three. Then you come up losing five."

Tim wasn't about to let deadbeats ride free on his car. He pondered the situation as the car chugged toward the Wharf, and when they stopped at Lombard Street he had an idea. He approached the tour group leader.

"How about a group photo at the crooked street?" he asked her.

"Sure. Sounds like fun." The woman herded her chattering charges off the car toward the sidewalk, where they all lined up with the bay view behind them.

And while they took their pictures, and the gripman fell over laughing, Tim walked back to the cable car and collected fares from the dozen or so people who weren't having their picture taken.

Often, disoriented tourists can be grateful that today's conductors <u>are</u> honest.

"That's for five of us." The man in the windbreaker motioned to the woman and three children next to him and handed Wendell a wad of bills folded in half.

"One way or all day?" Wendell asked. The man looked confused. "It's two dollars one way, six dollars for an all-day pass," Wendell explained for the two-hundredth time that day.

The man in the windbreaker leaned over to his wife and discussed the question at length. While he waited, Wendell unfolded the bills and began counting them.

"One way, I guess," the man decided finally.

"That'll be ten dollars," Wendell said. And he carefully handed back the wad of money — nine one-hundred-dollar bills.

Still, some of the old "they're-all-crooks" attitude persists — enough so that Muni, in its infinite wisdom, periodically sends out spies to ride the lines anonymously, checking up on them.

That's right, spies. They could be anyone — men in business suits, "tourists" in Bermuda shorts, little old ladies with shopping bags — riding the cable cars hoping to catch a conductor with sticky fingers.

To do this, of course, the spies need to be anonymous, which is why Muni outsources the task to private security agencies. But they neglected to factor in the resourcefulness of the average cable car operator.

Even the cable car people themselves don't know who it was or how he did it — at least, that's their story and they're sticking to it. But one of their number managed to get a set of photographs of an entire spy cadre. He pasted them up on a sheet of paper, ran it through a copy machine, and posted copies on the bathroom walls at the end of every cable car line.

"Oh, they had a fit up there," one conductor chortles. "They had an absolute witch hunt trying to find out who did it."

Is it necessary to state that they never did?

The spies are the main reason some conductors insist on seeing every single FastPass every single ride, even if the passenger is someone they see every day. Unfortunately, because too many locals don't realize this, it can be a source of tension. This is especially true on the Cal line, where the morning runs are filled with daily commuters. And it's one reason a certain number of conductors prefer to work the tourist-filled Powell lines.

Burton is one of them.

> "The folks over on the Cal line, they think they're prima donnas. You're supposed to know where they get off, whether they got a pass, the whole nine yards."

It was early morning and the cable car was about half-full when it pulled away from Van Ness heading for the Financial District. Burton moved to the front of the car and, as he did every morning, announced: "Good morning. Fares, please."

"Oh, come on." The woman in the business suit was juggling briefcase, purse, newspaper, and coffee. "You know all of us." She glared at him. "Why do you have to harrass us every morning by asking us to dig out our passes? We're the same people you see every day."

Across the bench, other regulars nodded. It was true; why did this guy keep insisting they haul out their wallets, or scrabble around in their purses, when he knew they had passes?

And Burton, fed up, went off on the lot of them.

"Wait a minute." He returned the glares impartially, looking from one passenger to the next. "My job description reads that I ask passengers for their fares. This is what I'm paid to do. And the people that I work for are serious about this. So serious that they have people who come out here in plain clothes, in all kinds of weather, just to make sure that I do this.

"Now you," he focused sternly on the woman who'd begun the insurrection, "and all these people here, I know have passes. You went down and bought the passes. Can you explain to me why you don't want to show them to me?

"So we're going to have to work this out. If you don't want to show me your pass, I tell you what I can do. I can get on the phone and explain your situation to the boss and have him send somebody out here. Is that what you want me to do?"

By the time he finished his soft-spoken tirade, the passengers were looking embarrassed. Burton paused, then said: "Okay. One, two, three — fares, please." And with sheepish grins, the commuters held up their FastPasses.

"The next morning," Burton recalls, laughing, "I stepped up on the car and every single one of them greeted me by waving their passes."

Of course, there are risks involved in dealing with large amounts of cash.

Cam had just finished a weekend run on the Cal line, scooping up fares as quickly as possible and stuffing the bills in his pocket. Now he was sitting on the outside bench thumbing through the take, counting and sorting. He never noticed the teenager on the bicycle — until the kid swooped past, grabbed the entire wad of bills from his hand, and disappeared from sight.

🚋 🚋 🚋

Jamal was conducting on the Hyde line, outbound from Market Street. He'd made his way through the crowded car, collected all the fares, and now he was standing in the doorway, casually arranging the bills as the cable car pulled out from the Powell-Sutter corner. The very, very windy Powell-Sutter corner...

Wooded park at Hyde and Greenwich Streets.

Jamal estimates that he managed to retrieve about half the take. "There were a lot of happy panhandlers downtown that day."

🚋 🚋 🚋

At Hyde and Greenwich, there's a park high atop the hill overlooking the cable car tracks. Matt's car was outbound late one night when he spotted the batch of kids.

"They must have been partying pretty hard," he recalls, "because they were pretty drunk."

As the cable car approached, the kids hooted and shouted, and as the car came abreast of the park, the whole batch of them turned their backs, dropped their pants, and mooned the car full of tourists.

Well, no big deal, but Matt knew they'd still be there on the ride back, and he had an idea.

When the car reached the turntable and loaded up with the next batch of tourists, he pulled a handful of rubber bands out of his pocket, the ones he used to wrap up wads of bills. He took a handful of receipts, tore them into strips, and folded them up real tight. Then he handed out this weaponry to the tourists on the right side of the car, along with a quick lesson on the art of the slingshot.

"Sure enough," Matt recalls, grinning, "when we came back up the hill there are these guys with their pants down around their legs."

The tourists did him proud. Half a dozen direct hits, and suddenly the mooners are yelping in pain. "Hey, what're you doing?" "Cut it out!"

"Now they're rubbing their asses and running for cover," Matt says, laughing. "And when we came back on the next trip, they were gone."

Us vs. Them

What tourists rarely see —
the machine shop
inside the cable car barn.

Nothing encapsulates the prevailing attitude of cable car operators toward Muni management better than this:

The afternoon that the burning truck rammed the tower, someone was relating the incident to a group of gripmen and conductors. He described Gavin, sitting blamelessly in the tower when he felt the impact. He told them how Gavin had leapt to his feet when he saw the flames, grabbed the fire extinguisher and raced outside. Then he described the damage to the rails surrounding the tower.

There was a brief pause while everyone absorbed the story. Then a conductor asked, deadpan: "Has Muni decided yet whether it was the gripman's fault?"

> "Do I have something against management? What management? They couldn't manage their own behinds."

The level of hostility between the operators and the "suits" is far more than just normal anti-management grousing. Their contempt for management is palpable.

The hostility reached unprecedented levels of nastiness recently when it entered the political arena. A city-wide referendum demanding improved Muni service was followed by investigations into municipal overtime pay. Suddenly, the hostility was being played out in public.

And as far as the operators were concerned, they were being made the public whipping boys for Muni's own incompetence.

No issue provoked as much bitterness as overtime, especially when a front-page newspaper story identified one operator, by name, as the third-highest-paid overtime worker in city government.

"They said we earn too much money," Harmon says bitterly, "but they never said how much time we spent away from home. We *earn* that money. This man spent almost 14 hours a day, seven days a week, over here."

"And if they don't pay overtime," he points out, "they're going to have even more shortages over here."

Stupid Bureaucracy Tricks

In the winter of 1999, the California line was shut down for three months for repairs, and replaced by buses. And initially, those buses were free.

"The thing is," Dana explains, "if someone gets on a bus and pays the fare, we have to give them a transfer. But they didn't give us drivers any transfers."

After a couple of weeks, several of the regulars began to complain. After all, they'd paid for their monthly FastPasses. Why should everyone else, especially tourists, ride free?

They had a point, Dana conceded. So he went to the cable car barn to discuss the matter with the dispatcher.

"I don't know," the dispatcher said. "Ask the supervisor."

Dana asked the supervisor. "Ask the dispatcher," the supervisor said.

"I don't know," the dispatcher repeated, and called the revenue office.

"Yes, of course riders are supposed to pay," the revenue office informed Dana.

"Well, then we need transfers," Dana explained.

"Oh, if you don't have transfers, don't have them pay." And the revenue officer, satisfied that the problem was solved, promptly hung up.

A cable car's track brakes are simply four chunks of very soft wood, exactly as designed by Andrew Hallidie. But back in the early sixties, a group of scientists thought they had a better idea.

"Oh, that was then," they dismissed the creator's decree. "We've come up with a material that'll stop those cars just like that, bang, even in the rain." And they displayed a milky-looking white plastic substance.

The Muni brain trust was impressed. They installed the miracle substance on a cable car; to simulate wet weather, they even added two tanks of water, with hoses running to the ground.

Brakes last approximately four days under good conditions. This one's time is up.

Then the Muni brain trust climbed aboard, en masse, and set out for a trial run.

Down the hill they went, picking up speed. At the appropriate moment, the gripman pulled the lever and applied the miracle brakes.

Friction ensued; the miracle substance heated up; and its surface rapidly turned to something resembling butter.

As the Muni brain trust clung to their poles in terror, the experienced gripman, with a look of deep disgust, threw the slot blade and wrestled the cable car to a halt.

And that's why cable car brakes are still four chunks of very soft wood.

The cable cars run from approximately six a.m. to 1 a.m., but the cable car barn never sleeps. When the cables are turned off for the night, maintenance crews take over.

Or at least, that was the theory, until the night someone noticed one of the shop crew in the barn, in his pajamas.

Turned out he was coming to the barn every night, clocking in, and then going back home — and back to bed for the night. Turned out further, he'd been doing it for five years.

Why hadn't anyone reported him? Because he wasn't the only one doing it. Seems a group of them had been taking turns getting paid for their good night's sleep.

Inspectors and Other Strangers

All bureaucracies have one thing in common — the less actual work an employee does, the more money he makes. A brilliant classroom teacher can only earn more money by abandoning the classroom and "moving up" to become an administrator. And a cable car operator can only earn more money by abandoning the cable cars and "moving up" to become an inspector.

Inspectors, recognizable by their navy blue uniforms, hang around at the ends of Muni lines. No one is quite sure what their actual function is, exactly. But to the average gripman, an inspector is kind of like having something in your eye — it annoys you for a while, but then you blink a couple of times and it goes away.

Nothing about Muni angers cable car operators more than a no-nothing inspector.

"When I first started here," Eli recalls, "you were required to weigh 180 pounds. I weighed 147. So I put on a lot of clothes, got the job, and went on a weight-gain diet. The first couple of months, my muscles were so beat up I couldn't put my hands in my back pocket." He grimaces over memories. "I worked that Hyde line on weekends, bumper to bumper traffic. I worked the most difficult cars there were. At the time I was the youngest guy in the division.

"Now all of a sudden here's some guy in a blue suit who's only been two years driving a bus, comes along and shakes a pencil at me. And I'm not taking anything off him. That's not arrogance, it's just ... " He shrugs. "I'm not taking it until he's gone through what I've gone through."

One continuous source of friction is headway — the length of time between cars.

"The company that runs the system has a *policy* that they don't like Muni operators."

For Muni, the magic number is usually six — that is, in an ideal world cable cars would run six minutes apart. The trouble is, given the shortage of qualified gripmen, that almost always requires more cable cars than there are available.

Unfortunately, too many inspectors don't make the connection.

"The guy was on a power trip," Derek says.

It takes a minimum of 40 minutes, under ideal conditions, for a cable car to complete a round trip on the Hyde line. On this particular morning, there were four cars running.

The inspector sent them out "on six" — six minutes apart.

Obediently, the gripmen did as they were told. All four cars pulled out and disappeared over the hill. And for nearly twenty minutes, there was not a single cable car in sight.

When Derek arrived back at the turntable, the inspector was gone.

🚃 🚃 🚃

Another unclear-on-the-concept inspector was bound and determined to shape up the Mason line. "Leave right behind the car in front of you," he'd order them. Or: "Leave as soon as you get to the turntable."

The gripmen decided to let him have his way.

"We just all shrugged, said 'no problem,' and did what he told us," Warner reports.

He laughs. "So you'd look up Columbus, and there'd be six cars — brrrrrrrr — like a railroad train, one after the other. And then about forty minutes later, six cars come outbound, brrrrrrrrr.

"And a couple of days after that, he said, 'I can't deal with this' and left."

And then there was the inspector they referred to as Six-Minute Simon.

"It's hard to run cars every six minutes if you're missing four cars out of ten," Lamar points out. But that's what Six-Minute Simon wanted.

Lamar had barely pulled his car to a stop at Hyde and Beach when Simon came hustling over. Passengers were still getting off the car as he announced: "I want you to leave right now."

"At least let the people off the car first," Lamar said.

"Yeah, yeah." Simon waited with barely-concealed impatience.

As the last passenger stepped off, so did Lamar. He walked around to the front of the car. He picked up a newspaper. He looked at Simon.

"Seven oh two," he said.

A 702 is Muni code for "personal necessity" — meaning a bathroom break. A 702 is non-negotiable, even by Six-Minute Simon.

Lamar repeated once more, loudly: "Seven oh two." Then he went into the bathroom and sat there. For fifteen minutes.

"By the time I came out, he was ready to explode," Lamar says, "but there was nothing he could do about it. And it meant the three guys behind me got some sort of break, too.

"After that," he reports says, "all the guys were instructed to take seven oh twos."

And then there are the other petty tyrannies of the minor bureaucrat.

"I've been a gripman for twenty-five years," Milo says, "and I hadn't been written up since 1982." He snorts in disgust. "On this run my leaving time is seven-forty. Last year I pulled out one day at seven-forty-two, and this brand-new inspector wrote me up. For leaving two minutes late."

"One day I was delayed by a garbage truck," Lief recalls. "As soon as I was able to move I went on as fast as I could. But I had to make my stops, pick up my regulars, and I got written up for being late."

There was the inspector who was positive certain gripmen were running the double-X mandatory stops. This one took it into his head to hide in a nearby garage with a camera, hoping to get the supposed miscreants on film.

And the one who was convinced that certain conductors were pocketing fares. He took to boarding cable cars and going through the car asking passengers to show their receipts.

And then there was the one who ... "I swear I am not making this up," Les grins at the memory.

At the foot of each line is a small bathroom for operators to use. And at the Hyde Street turntable, there's an extra amenity — a tiny chamber with just enough room for one person, a mini-refrigerator, and one or two other bits and pieces, including a coffeepot.

On this day, someone happened to mention how grungy the coffeemaker was. And to everyone's surprise, the inspector, McGonigle, volunteered to take it into the bathroom and clean it.

The operators' shed at the Hyde Street turntable.

To their even greater surprise, he emerged with the coffeemaker in bright, shiny-clean condition.

"McGonigle, you did a great job," someone exclaimed. "How'd you get it so clean?"

"Oh, it was easy," McGonigle replied. "There was a brush right there in the bathroom and I just used that."

Lest you think that the general hostility toward inspectors is simply an anti-authority bias, check out Car Number 60, on the California line. There you'll see a metal plaque actually dedicated to an inspector, with the complete approval of the operators.

"He was one of the good guys," Marshall recalls. "He was the kind of guy who got everybody's respect because when we were out here in the summertime trying to keep the line on time, just running all day long, trying to maintain the schedule they had us run on, when we were out here getting our butts kicked, he would purposely slow the line down and put it on twelve-minute headways just to give us a break. So if he needed a favor we didn't hesitate to help him out. He was a good guy; that's why he's got his plaque on the cable car."

The Ziggy Files

In the words of one gripman: "Ziggy was the only guy ever to get his name on the bathroom wall and the roll of toilet paper in one week."

No one, before or since, has been as thoroughly despised; no one ever contributed as much to cable car operators' solidarity. On some cable cars, you can still see hand-made stickers with the name inside the red circle-and-slash symbol for "No Ziggy."

No inspector was ever driven away from the cable car lines faster.

Remember — there are not enough people who can do this job. Within the memory of anyone now working the cable cars, there have never been enough qualified gripmen to fully staff every line every day. The only way they keep running is because operators are willing to work overtime. And RDO — Regular Day Off — work is entirely optional.

If Ziggy was working a line, there were no RDOs.

"If somebody was supposed to work California Street," Kevin recalls, "they'd refuse if Ziggy was there. Whatever line he was on, they weren't going to work, period. And then the guys ending their regular shifts, instead of them saying, well, I'll do an extra four-hour piece, they pulled in." He grins. "A few times they ended up sending out buses because they couldn't keep the cable cars running."

The Day The Cal Line Pulled In

On Sundays, with no commuters to carry and no Fisherman's Wharf destination, the California line is the cable car stepchild, the last line to be staffed. On this summer Sunday afternoon, there are only three cars working the line.

For reasons unknown, Ziggy is stationed at California and Drumm. For reasons equally unknown, he orders the three gripmen to head out six minutes apart.

Now, it takes a *minimum* of 38 minutes to complete a run from Drumm to Van Ness and back again. Unfortunately, "do the math" isn't a concept Ziggy can handle. The gripmen try to explain it to him, but Ziggy just grumbles and repeats his orders.

Zeke, in the lead car, calls central control to explain the problem.

"Never mind," he's told peremptorily. "Just do what the inspector tells you."

Zeke, who's working RDO, isn't having any. "The hell with that," he declares. "Just cancel my time off the clock. I'm pulling in and going home."

And now there are two — only two cable cars on the entire Cal line. And *still* Ziggy continues to order them out on six.

Brent, next in line, is coming to the end of his regular shift, due to be relieved on his next trip out. But when he checks with dispatch, he's informed there's no relief available. How about working overtime? he's asked.

Brent hedges; first, he calls Erwin, Ziggy's boss.

"Ziggy's doing his job," Erwin snaps. "And you guys should just shut up and do yours." Then he makes his fatal mistake. "We're going to whip the cable cars into shape," he says.

Brent, who has a short fuse at the best of times, goes ballistic. He screams into the phone for a couple of minutes; then he calls dispatch and informs them that he'll work an extra shift at approximately the time there's snowboarding in hell. Then he gets back on his empty cable car and, still screaming, heads uphill to turn in his car and go home.

And then there was one — one last cable car, whose operators, also at the end of their shift, pull out a few minutes later for their last run, leaving Ziggy the triumphant monarch of an empty cable car line.

"They have no idea they're in the transportation business. Passengers mean nothing to them, employee relationships mean nothing to them, they're all just thinking about their next promotion."

Once, in a previous life, Ziggy had been a cable car conductor — for all of five months. Now, of course, he is an inspector, a word he apparently translates as "expert."

The dies inside the grip — the jaws that close over the cable — are made of soft metal, for reasons too technical to go into here. And so grips wear out; the average grip is replaced every three or four days. This is perfectly normal.

Bernie had a bad grip. He finished his run down to the end of Hyde Street, called central control in the ordinary way, and asked for the truck to come out and replace it.

Central control's response was not ordinary.

"There's an inspector down there on the scene," Bernie was told. "He can make the call."

"Say what?" Bernie sputtered.

Enter Ziggy, who climbed onto the cable car and looked down into the grip hole. He took hold of the grip handle and shook it. Then he called central control:

"There's nothing wrong with this grip," he told them. "It's a good grip."

Even now, Bernie shakes his head in disbelief. "He had the nerve to shake the grip and say there's nothing wrong with it? Even I can't do that, and I've been gripping for 20 years. And this guy's never gripped in his life."

Luckily, before Bernie could inflict grievous bodily harm, a different inspector came on the radio and informed central: "That's not the inspector's call to make."

"I actually wrote Ziggy up," Colin recalls gleefully.

Conducting on the Cal line one summer Sunday, Colin had collected fistfuls of money, which he'd crammed into his pocket while the car was moving. At the end of the run, the car was sitting in the waiting area at Drumm, and Colin had the piles of cash spread out on the seat inside the compartment while he sorted and arranged it.

The car in front of him had just pulled out from the plaza alongside the Hyatt Regency on its next run, which meant that Colin had ten minutes before his car was due to follow.

Enter Ziggy.

Ziggy, for some reason, ordered them to take the car across Drumm to the plaza and load up passengers immediately. The operators could do their waiting over there.

"We'll take it over as soon as I've done my money." Colin indicated the stacks of money — money he was personally responsible for.

"Take it over now," Ziggy insisted. "I'm giving you a direct order."

Werner, the gripman, looked at Colin and cocked his head.

"Werner, do not move this car," Colin said, and to Ziggy: "I've got my money lying all over the seat, and I'm not going across with it like this."

"I don't care," Ziggy said with the stubbornness of the truly clueless. "I gave you a direct order."

"I told you I'd take it over when I'm finished," Colin snapped. "If you can't accept that, you can call it in, or you can get off the car. Or else," he said, finally fed up, "you can stay on the car, or do whatever you want, because I'm writing you up."

"And that's just what I did," Colin reports with satisfaction. "And after that we didn't see Ziggy no more."

Fighting Back

The difference between bus drivers and cable car operators is simple: it's a lot easier to find new bus drivers.

Unlike buses, cable cars aren't plug-and-play. Which means that, in a pinch, Muni can't hire temporary workers; most important, they can't hire scabs.

Wildcat Strikes

"There aren't too many people who can do this job," Trey reiterates. "And we've had a lot of wildcat strikes over here, where we've told them exactly that.

"What that accomplished is that management had to come down and talk to us and work it out. Whereas with the bus drivers, they just run right over those guys, and then replace them if they complain."

Cable car people divide time into two periods — before and after the Shutdown. In 1982, after decades of neglect, the entire cable car system was shut down for two years of total renovation, from the underground channels on up. Gripmen who predate the Shutdown still get angry recalling the dilapidated condition of the system they had to operate.

Silas was gripping inbound on California Street when his cable car hit a defective depression beam at Kearny. The force of the impact hurled him through the front window and onto the street. The cable car started to roll backward; Silas picked himself up, managed to climb back aboard, and wrestled the cable car to a halt. Then he passed out.

Trey was just about to pull out on his Mason line run when the word came down about the accident.

"We heard there was this bad accident on California Street, but we were getting conflicting stories — you know, he was hurt bad, he was killed, nobody knew. So I headed outbound on the Mason line. When I got to Bay and Taylor, I told the guys there: I don't know about you, but I'm pulling in. Everybody followed me, and once we got back to the barn, we got all the Hyde line to pull in, and came up and got all the California cars to pull in. So all three lines walked out that night, until we found out that Silas was okay."

If the cable cars can't run without gripmen, it can't run without conductors, either. One of the Muni suits forgot this fact the day he decided to score points with a public statement accusing them of thievery. The conductors, he proclaimed, were using the cable cars as "their own

The sheaves that operate the cables inside the barn.

personal piggy bank." Shortly thereafter, the piggy bank was closed as every conductor in the division joined in a demonstration at Powell and Market.

Working the Media

Operators also tend to be fairly media-savvy.

It was back before the Shutdown, after a particularly horrific accident in the barn which resulted in the deaths of two cable maintenance workers. Everyone knew the system was deteriorating; no one knew how badly.

Shell decided it was time to find out.

"Me and two other guys went out there," Shell recalls. "We started at Jackson and Mason, and walked the Mason line outbound."

All along the route, the three men stopped at each hatch cover, lifted it, and looked inside to check the equipment under the street. What they found was, to put it politely, a mess.

"There were pulleys missing, there were pieces broken, there were pulleys frozen so that the cable was just running through and cutting them in half." They made a note of each piece of defective equipment, replaced the hatch cover, and continued their walk.

They never made it to the end of the line.

Somebody — Shell doesn't say who — had called the TV stations, and when they reached Columbus, they were met by a news crew.

And immediately after that, they were met by an inspector, who ordered them to stop.

"They definitely didn't want us to know any more," Shell reports drily.

But it wasn't long afterward that the entire system was shut down for two years' worth of renovation.

🚋 🚋 🚋

Seth was the conductor who stopped the runaway cable car after it was rammed by a suicidal driver. But when he asked for a few days off to recover, the supervisor rejected his request.

"Let's just say this guy wasn't what you'd call operator-friendly," Seth deadpans.

"Okay," Seth told him. "I guess I'll go talk to Channel 4, and Channel 5, and Channel 7. And I'll tell them that I'm the guy who saved all those people, and now you won't even let me have a day off."

"And the supervisor very generously came around," Seth reports ironically.

Working the System

But the most basic way that operators gain control over their own work lives is simply by using what they know best — the cable cars themselves.

"It's pretty easy to tie up a line," Angelo points out. "On these cable cars, you can always find something wrong somewhere."

And in a pinch, there's always that red emergency handle — the slot blade.

In order to run properly, the cable is lubricated. But too much lube, and the grip is almost impossible to control.

On this day, the cable was over-lubed, so badly that gripmen feared for their passengers, not to mention themselves.

"The operators were trying to convey this, and the powers-that-be didn't want to listen," Angelo reports. "They told us: you just keep working, everything is fine." He grins. "Okay, no problem."

Shortly thereafter, a cable car lost the grip at Washington and Mason, right at the juncture of both Fisherman's Wharf lines. Well, what's a gripman to do?

Throw the slot blade, of course.

A few minutes later, another gripman was forced to throw a blade at Mason and Union Streets. That shut down the Mason line. And a few minutes after that, a California line car threw a blade at Powell.

"There's no way in the world you can prove we're doing something wrong," Angelo says innocently. "It's an emergency; you've gotta pull the slot blade."

Result: all three lines went down. Second result: the cable was fixed.

Of course, there are times when playing it by the book is the smart-money choice.

There are all sorts of excitements in San Francisco, but few match the thrill of finding a legal parking place. So the driver of the car at Hyde and Northpoint may be forgiven for a mental lapse. He'd stopped when he saw a car pulling out of a spot, then backed up to give it room — and backed right into Zeke's cable car.

The driver looked over his shoulder, made complicated hand motions, and pulled into the parking spot. A beat cop, who happened to be walking by, took the particulars, and when they were done the driver walked away down the hill.

Just another fender-bender; and since Zeke had the guy's license number and a batch of witnesses, he didn't worry overmuch about it.

Except, when they were gone, he walked over to the car and took down the VIN number to make sure his report was absolutely complete.

"It's called covering your ass," Zeke says drily. "Because if I don't, sure as hell, the next morning five members of the Slobbovian drug dealers association'll be there with neck braces on."

🚋 🚋 🚋

Todd was on the Cal line, coming down the steep hill from Stockton to Grant, when one car cut off another, and both stopped directly in front of him. Todd immediately hit the track brake.

Instead of stopping, the cable car began to pick up speed.

Without hesitation, Todd threw the slot blade and halted the cable car, inches from the two cars. At which point, the cars drove away.

While he waited for the truck to free his slot blade, Todd decided something about the incident didn't feel right. It was a San Francisco rarity, a perfectly clear, sunny day with no rain or fog, so why had his wheels slipped?

He stepped down and ran his fingers along the tracks. Sure enough, he felt a slick, oily substance smeared on the tracks, extending nearly twenty feet forward.

"It's an insurance scam," Todd explains. "One car gets in front of a truck or a bus and slows down until it's close to his rear bumper. Then a confederate pulls in front of him and cuts him off." He nods knowingly. "So the guy has to slam on his brakes and of course the truck rear-ends him. Then they collect from the insurance company." He grins. "But not that day."

And if all that doesn't work, well, you just learn to wait them out.

Now it has already been established that cable cars tend to attract extroverts. And these extroverts, like so many other San Franciscans, just naturally enjoy dressing up. So on the day before Christmas, many operators wear Santa suits. On Hallowe'en, costumes dot the cars. And on New Year's Eve at the turn of the millennium, one gripman-conductor pair worked their shift in full, glorious evening wear, right down to the patent-leather shoes.

On a more regular basis, many cable car operators mark out their individuality via headgear. They may wear 49er caps, or berets, or a leather fedora, or even a pith helmet.

And every now and then some new honcho decides to show the cable car operators who's the boss by throwing the uniform regs at them.

Now uniform regs, as any gripman will tell you, are designed for bus drivers. They are not designed for men who work outdoors in all weather, standing on their feet, throwing their muscles against intractable machinery.

Nor are they designed for individualists.

"The thing about Muni," Linc explains, "is that they pass down these rules and regulations but they don't plan on enforcing these rules and regulations." He grins. "If you're smart, you'll just keep your mouth shut for a while. You say okay, and you adhere to the rules and regulations for a couple of weeks, then you go back to doing what you were doing."

Equipment-Caused Accidents

Even after complete renovation, cable car machinery isn't foolproof. As with any system, things can go wrong. Luckily tourists, bless them, will often take the cable car experience at face value, unaware that roaring downhill and zooming through intersections is not business as usual.

It had all the necessary elements for disaster — a fully-loaded cable car, a persistent light rain, and the Chestnut Street hill heading down the long, long grade to Bay. That's where Tark's car chose to lose the cable.

"It just fell out of the grip," Tark recalls. "The car just took off, and we couldn't stop for two and a half blocks."

Tark figures if they'd pulled the slot blade at that speed passengers would have ponged off the car like pinballs. He pulled it finally when they crossed Northpoint, and even there, he says, it took a couple of car lengths to stop the car.

"You lose the cable on the Hyde Street hill with a light rain and it's over — you're going for a sledding trip, and that's what happened."

He shakes his head. "Not only was nobody hurt, but people were saying: Hey, let's do it again." He laughs. "They didn't know. Some of the kids were saying, wow, I never knew it was as fast as that. They wanted to go down again."

It was, Jake points out, a Friday the Thirteenth.

He had just crossed Northpoint and was preparing to stop at the end of the Hyde line. He hauled back on the brake handle, preparing to stop.

And found himself flat on his back, staring up at the ceiling, clutching a chunk of the brake handle that had snapped clean off in his hand.

The cable car, of course, kept moving until it slammed into the next car, which slammed into the next car, which slammed into the next.

"We pushed three cars about twenty-five feet, and it caused thousands of dollars worth of damage," Jake reports. "Afterward, they put new handles on all the brakes on all the cable cars.

"I also had to talk to the national traffic safety board," he says. "And of course I was told: You know what to say, don't you?"

If going from a dead stop to nine miles an hour is dangerous, going from nine miles an hour to a dead stop is even worse.

That's what happened to Roland's car at California and Hyde.

It was their first run of the morning, and Roland was conducting. Neither he nor the gripman realized that the car ahead of theirs had dropped a small bolt from its underside. Not an important bolt; and in the normal run of things its absence would have been noticed and corrected on the next inspection.

This time, the bolt was discovered the hard way.

It had rolled across the track and wedged itself into the cable slot, the one the grip rides through. Wedged itself in so tightly, in fact, that when Roland's grip reached it, the cable car came to an instant stop.

"It was like running into a brick wall," Roland recalls. "The gripman cracked a couple of ribs, but I was at the back, close to the doorway, so when it stopped I just grabbed the door frame and went on through. I had my arms out so I was able to cushion my flight through the car."

And then there are strands.

"The cable" is actually six cables, each made of fifteen strands of twisted steel wire, wrapped around a core of rope. The cable, as a whole, doesn't break; but individual strands do. And a broken strand, left to its own devices, will whip itself into a huge, tangled knot as it races along under the street.

Eventually, this knot can become big enough, and strong enough, to shove forward everything in its path. Including cable cars.

Nowadays, there are "strand detectors" that signal the barn as soon as a single broken strand occurs, automatically shutting down the line. But in the past, broken strands have produced some fairly spectacular accidents.

The most famous occurred on Powell, when a huge ball of twisted wire rammed into the grip of a cable car between O'Farrell and Ellis, shoving it forward down the line. When the dust settled, four cars were crumpled together at the Market Street turntable.

An unchecked strand can wind intself into a knot a hundred feet long, as a group of operators on the Cal line remember only too well.

There were three cable cars in the layover area at California and Drumm, and five of the operators were gathered in the last one in line. Jason wasn't among them; he'd stepped off the lead car for a quick fuel-up from a nearby coffee shop, leaving the grip open but not dropping the cable.

The group in the rear car heard a thumping sound. They looked up casually, wondering what it was.

What they saw was the lead cable car moving away from them, at full cable speed, with no one at the grip.

As all five of them raced toward the runaway car, Jason emerged from the coffee shop, juggling orange juice and coffee and a bag of donuts. He goggled for a split second at the sight of his empty cable car being chased by a clutch of operators; then, realizing at once that it had to be a strand, he took off in pursuit.

Unfortunately, he was so unnerved that he didn't quite have the presence of mind to drop what he was carrying. He caught up with the cable car all right; only he couldn't quite manage to get on with his hands full.

It was another gripman who finally jumped aboard and wrestled the car to a stop just inches short of the bumper bar.

Management at Muni
By a Gripman

Management at Muni is a sight that you must see,
    Before this topheavy bureaucracy slides into the sea.
They have at least one manager for every two of us,
    No wonder you can never find someone to drive a bus.
Promotions based on who you know or how well you kiss ass,
    Don't dare make a decision or their test you'll never pass.
Show no personal initiative and don't think on your feet,
    Or you'll be right back here with us, driving down the street.
A few good ones do sneak through and help the railway work,
    I don't know how they stand to work with mostly bleeping jerks.
Our defense budget's rivaled by the money Muni wastes,
    Just what they pissed away last year would put a bus in space.
I can see its orbit now, around and round she goes,
    And they've got the same old problem there, the doors will never close.
I've read Muni memos Einstein couldn't figure out,
    Creating useless paper's what their job is all about.
Shop against the drivers is what they must promote,
    If we ever get together then we'll have them by the throat.
They must divide to conquer — that's the plan that they have thought,
    Keep us on each others' ass or else their scam's been caught.
Management is always right — it's all the driver's fault,
    They can screw us both at once, that's what it's all about.
Riders must hate drivers for this plan to stay in place,
    "Everything's the driver's fault" must always be their case.
Metro cars and signal systems designed and made in hell,
    This is all the driver's fault? Somehow that story smells.
Given what we work with, what we do is most astounding,
    Day after day, year after year, and still we take a pounding.
Management has never stood behind us when attacked,
    They're too busy sticking knives in everybody's back.
Soon I'll be gone, retiring soon, you'll see no more of me,
    Then this topheavy bureaucracy can slip into the sea.

© by the gripman who wrote it

About the author

Susan Holtzer is the author of seven mystery novels
from St. Martin's Press, featuring Anneke Haagen and
former Pittsburgh Steelers linebacker Karl Genesko.
She and her husband live in San Francisco, where
their only regret is that no cable car line runs out to
Candlestick Park.